DATE DUE

INTRODUCTION TO ART THERAPY

ABOUT THE AUTHOR

Bruce L. Moon, Ph.D., ATR-BC, is a professor and chair of the art therapy department at Mount Mary College in Milwaukee, Wisconsin. He is the 2007 recipient of the Honorary Life Member (HLM) award of the American Art Therapy Association. Formerly the director of the graduate program at Marywood University in Scranton, Pennsylvania, and the Harding Graduate Clinical Art Therapy Program in Worthington, Ohio, he has extensive clinical, administrative, and teaching experience. He holds a doctorate in creative arts with specialization in art therapy from Union Institute in Cincinnati, Ohio. Doctor Moon's current clinical practice is focused on the treatment of emotionally disturbed adolescents. He has lectured and led workshops at many colleges, universities, conferences, and symposia in the United States and Canada.

Doctor Moon is the author of *Existential Art Therapy: The Canvas Mirror; Essentials of Art Therapy Training and Practice; Art and Soul: Reflections on an Artistic Psychology; The Dynamics of Art as Therapy with Adolescents; Ethical Issues in Art Therapy;* and *The Role of Metaphor in Art Therapy: Theory, Method, and Experience.* He is editor of *Working with Images: The Art of Art Therapists* and co-editor of *Word Pictures: The Poetry and Art of Art Therapists.* Moon's many years of experience in clinical and educational settings, coupled with his interdisciplinary training in art education, art therapy, theology, and creative arts, inspire his provocative theoretical and practical approach to the discipline of art therapy.

Author's Note

The clinical vignettes in this book are, in spirit, true. In all instances, details are fictional to ensure the confidentiality of persons with whom I have worked. The case illustrations and artworks presented are amalgamations of many specific situations. My intention is to provide realistic accounts of an art therapist's work while also protecting the privacy of individuals.

Second Edition

INTRODUCTION TO ART THERAPY

Faith in the Product

By

BRUCE L. MOON, Ph.D., ATR-BC

With Forewords by

Shaun McNiff

CHARLES C THOMAS • PUBLISHER, LTD.
Springfield • Illinois • U.S.A.

Published and Distributed Throughout the World by

CHARLES C THOMAS • PUBLISHER, LTD.
2600 South First Street
Springfield, Illinois 62794-9265

© 2008 by CHARLES C THOMAS • PUBLISHER, LTD.

ISBN 978-0-398-07796-9 (hard)
ISBN 978-0-398-07797-6 (paper)

Library of Congress Catalog Card Number: 2007040404

With THOMAS BOOKS *careful attention is given to all details of manufacturing
and design. It is the Publisher's desire to present books that are satisfactory as to their
physical qualities and artistic possibilities and appropriate for their particular use.*
THOMAS BOOKS *will be true to those laws of quality that assure a good name
and good will.*

Printed in the United States of America
MM-R-3

Library of Congress Cataloging in Publication Data

Moon, Bruce, L.
  Introduction to art therapy : faith in the product / by Bruce L. Moon; with
forwords by Shaun McNiff–2nd ed.
    p. cm.
  Includes bibliographical references and index.
  ISBN 978-0-398-07796-9 (hard)–ISBN 978-0-398-07797-6 (pbk.)
  1. Art therapy. I. Title.
  [DNLM: 1. Art Therapy. 2. Profesional-Patient Relations. WM 450.5.A8
M818i 2008]

RC489.A7M663 2008
615.89'1656–dc22   2007040404

This book is dedicated to Don Jones, ATR, HLM:
my mentor, colleague, hero, and friend.

Don Jones

FOREWORD

The 1994 edition of Bruce Moon's *Introduction to Art Therapy: Faith in the Product* has become a classic text in art therapy. I am leaving my original foreword intact because it is part of the historical record of the publication, and because it offers readers the passionate and enthusiastic response of another person's initial engagement of the book. In this foreword to the second edition, which updates and renews Moon's overview of art therapy, I will comment on the book's impact and Moon's larger influence in this field.

Since he began to focus on communicating his ideas and practice in books, starting with *Existential Art Therapy: The Canvas Mirror,* Moon has made major enduring contributions to art therapy. Because his writings are accessible, clear, convincing, and inspiring, he has pioneered and shaped the future direction of the discipline. I predict that time will recognize Moon as one of the most influential figures in the history of art therapy because of his many years of experience; the numbers of people whom he has directly influenced as an art therapist and educator; his consummate devotion to this work; and most importantly, the lasting power of his vision of art and healing.

The area within art therapy that has changed most significantly since the 1994 publication of this book is the realm that received the most critical attention in the first edition. At that time, Moon questioned the one-sided orientation to scientific justification that historically had permeated the art therapy field. As mentioned in my original foreword, art therapy's artistic identity took on a shadow dimension as the discipline aspired to cloak itself in science. The change we see today whereby art therapy celebrates and furthers its core artistic nature is largely due to the impact that Moon has had in calling for an art-based approach to practice and understanding in art therapy. I believe that the artistic soul of this work has become its most defining and appealing characteristic rather than an area of perceived inferiority in relation to what Moon describes as the "scientist-clinician" model.

Creative expression and the making of art objects are the empirical elements that characterize every approach to art therapy. They are our primary defining qualities: the unique things that we bring to the larger domains of therapy, healing, and wellness. An appreciation and recognition of art therapy's unique integration of art, psychology, and service to others have required neither the making of dichotomies between art and science nor doubts about the valuable roles that science and scientists can play in the art therapy field. An issue that Moon addresses in the first edition of this book is the one-sided scientism that has threatened the art-based powers of our discipline. Like Nietzsche and other expansive thinkers, Moon believes in the integration of complementary elements like art and science rather than the oppositional stances that attempt to reduce one to the other.

Thanks to Moon and others who have helped to establish a new mainstream in art therapy that affirms an essential basis in art, we are now in a clearer, more mature position to continue our discipline's historic partnership with science. With our artistic identities established and affirmed, we can confidently enter a new period of creation and growth in which more attention can be given to studying and perfecting the essential phenomena of art therapy.

The revisions in this new edition of *Introduction to Art Therapy: Faith in the Product* amplify the already large impact of a seminal text. Enhancements include: an overview of the spectrum of theoretical orientations within art therapy; a brief history of practice in the United States; descriptions of applications that were not widely understood in 1994; and most importantly, Moon's most current and seasoned descriptions of how he perceives the art therapy experience. A pragmatic and excellent teacher, Moon takes to heart and learns from his ongoing interactions with students at Mount Mary College and other settings, as evidenced by new issues and trends that he addresses in this book.

Art therapy continues to fascinate and inspire many of us over sustained periods of time and lengthy careers because of its one-of-a-kind integration of multiple forms of expression and human understanding. In my opinion, Moon remains one of the most intelligent and passionate contributors to this more complete vision and practice of art therapy. I am proud to be closely connected to his work and grateful for once again being asked to comment on this important book.

SHAUN MCNIFF
Professor and Dean of Lesley University
Cambridge, Massachusetts

FOREWORD TO THE FIRST EDITION

Introduction to Art Therapy: Faith in the Product offers Bruce Moon's most passionate and convincing call for the renewal of art therapy. The book is full of the inspiration and wisdom conveyed when a pioneer honestly describes his deepest personal instincts and those of art. More than any other book in art therapy literature, this text fulfills Rudolf Arnheim's (1972) ideal of a psychology of art permeated by smells of the studio. All of my senses were aroused as I read Moon's descriptions of clients working with diverse materials: the sounds of a man chiseling concrete, cutting and bending tin, building stretchers and preparing canvas, and squeezing wet clay. The clear and numerous vignettes show how art therapy is about action, constructing things, and making soul. I am intrigued by the subtitle *Faith in the Product* because the book is so strongly focused on "trusting the process." But process and product are two sides of a coin, necessary partners in creation that depend upon one another.

The embrace of products is an expression of a love and respect for images that is the foundation for art therapy's rediscovery of its soul. Moon helps us see the enduring therapeutic function of art: the healing that comes from making objects, perfecting craft, and reflecting upon the images as talismans who change the lives of those who are able to enter into relationships with them. *Faith in the Product* assumes that the image has a therapeutic purpose and offers medicine to those capable of being open to its remedies. This shift of authority from therapist to image threatens the control of the labeling mind that has until recently dominated the modern history of art therapy. Moon reintroduces art therapy to itself and suggests that closer attention to the deep streams of creation that run through our lives will help us realize ways of practicing art therapy that lie beyond our current imaginings.

Many professional art therapists distance themselves from art and strive to become scientists. One-sided identification with science and the repression of the artistic persona produce a malady that Pat Allen (1992) calls the "clinification syndrome." She attributes the malady to a self-defeating inferiority, which can be distinguished from the soul-deepening sense of vulnerability and humility that characterize Moon's work. The suppression of art paradoxically makes a shadow of the profession's essence because it threatens the tightly constructed and controlled persona of the therapeutic technician. The primal and unpredictable forces of creation do not fit the guise of the "in-control" scientific clinician. This contrast accounts for the hostility that often characterizes the institutional art therapy response to the soulful expressions of therapists who identify with the artist archetype. Unfortunately, this aggression is also addressed by the images and results in the "imagicide" that Moon (1995) laments. Images and products are vital parts of the constellation forming the shadow complex of art therapy. If we art therapists do not make, love, and honor our own images, how can we do this for our clients? When will we see that our profession is an ancient and also new collaboration between art and therapy that presages a transformation of both?

My sense of the shadow aspect of art therapy is not a matter of good and bad qualities, and it affects everyone involved in the profession. Exploration of the shadow is a mature and deeply affirming gesture not to be confused with the oppositionalism and bickering that characterize efforts to exercise control and power over professional affairs. Moon is not concerned with regulating others or institutionalizing his experience. He simply strives to describe his experience and maintain the freedom to practice according to his personal vision of art and healing. Since Moon worked for many years as an artist within a medical environment with scientist colleagues, he demonstrates how respect for art does not require opposition to science. However, the power of his medicine comes from his primary identity as an artist who offers something pure and unique to the therapeutic milieu.

The shadow of art therapy can be imagined as the antithesis of the face our profession displays to the world, the qualities that we hide. Moon articulates how he became caught up in this repression of the artistic persona. As long as the dominant energy of a profession represses a vital part of itself, it is impossible for any of us to avoid collusion until we are ready to openly admit to discomfort.

Moon says that for over 20 years, he denied the ideas that he presents in this book. But the denial is not his alone. He carries, lives out, and liberates the collective experience of our profession. The angels and demons of creation are always a step ahead of the reflecting mind. Moon (1994) says, "I did not want to hear them, nor did I want to speak them aloud for fear of the repercussions" (p. ix). Just as the individual ego fights against its shadow, the collective ego of a profession guards against whatever it deems unacceptable to its persona. Whoever has the courage to expose and celebrate the repressed shadow can expect an uneven reception. It takes time for these internal inclinations to mature "from inaudible murmurs to clear voices" that Moon (1994, p. ix) offers our profession.

We know from depth psychology that repression of the essential desires of the soul will ultimately generate a primal release of energy. Throughout this book, I feel the continuous bursting of the creative essence of art therapy. There seems to be no end to the corrective medicine, and Moon models how the transformation of a profession can occur with the precision and discipline that is also associated with the artist's craft. The outburst of passion is paired with aesthetic sensitivity and the containment of media.

This book will inspire serious artists to become involved in art therapy, and it will help art therapy students become more demanding consumers who ask, "Where is the art in my training and practice?" The book will also encourage veteran art therapists to renew their vocations by living the process of art therapy, which will help us become more effective in reaching others.

Moon's writing is pervaded by compassion and reverence for the sacred medicine of art. He gives testimony, bears witness, and does not try to prove anything; by doing this, he makes the book especially convincing and useful. He offers a new paradigm for art therapy practice, a contagious faith based on personal experience as an artist and therapist. He is not compromised or sidetracked by trying to prove the unprovable. This book contains inspirations and meditations on the healing function of art in which the shaping of an artistic product is a metaphor for a corresponding crafting of soul. The therapeutic studio is presented as a sanctuary where "confessions, thanksgiving, and praises" are expressed through images, and where it is all witnessed by the therapist who acts as a caretaker of the environment in which art heals. People are vital contributors to this therapeutic ecology, but they step aside to let art do its work.

This homage for the sacred dimension of art therapy shows yet another shadow repressed by the scientist/clinician persona. Moon's affirmation of *faith* is perhaps more provocative than his assertion of art's healing function. He not only challenges secular boundaries of art and science, but also mixes the more explosive materials of sacred and profane. Where pre-Freudian society repressed sexuality, the post-Freudian therapeutic world has considered spiritual experience off-limits, thus increasing its shadow power. Moon, who earned a master of divinity degree at the same time that he was becoming an art therapist, has never compromised his vision of art as soul's medicine. I feel the pulse of the sacred *Imago* in this book like nothing else Moon has written. By describing the intimate details of how he interacts with his clients, Moon shares the ministerial function he was destined to serve and affirms his faith in the creative spirit.

The many examples of Moon's practice at Harding Hospital and other clinical settings are straightforward, and they show how the making of art will adapt to the person's needs and offer guidance, insight, and revitalization. Art is part of living, and Moon repeatedly shows how the creative process cultivates the soulfulness of existence. Love, as Moon suggests, has got everything "to do with it." This book portrays art therapy as an image of the beloved, which Moon carries within his soul. The reader who is able to open and become a client of art's medicine will be transformed, as will art therapy itself. This vision of art therapy is an expression of a love for the soul, a love for creation. It is an introduction to art therapy that the profession needs more than ever, a fresh perspective of what we are about that respectfully acknowledges what art has always been. This is what I love about Moon's work and this book.

SHAUN McNIFF
Dean of Lesley University
Cambridge, Massachusetts

REFERENCES

Allen, P. B. (1992). Artist-in-residence: An alternative to "clinification" for art thera-pists. *Art Therapy: Journal of the American Art Therapy Association, 9*(1), pp. 22–28.

Arnheim, R. (1972). *Toward a psychology of art.* Los Angeles: University of California Press.

Moon, B. L. (1995). *Existential art therapy: The canvas mirror.* Springfield, IL: Charles C Thomas.

PREFACE

I am never entirely sure where or when my ideas emerge; they just come to me. The ideas presented in this book have developed subtly, gently, and fiercely. They have grown over the past 35 years from inaudible murmurs to clear voices within. For a long time, I tried to ignore these voices, and I denied their existence and relationship to me. Neither did I want to hear them, nor did I want to speak them aloud for fear of the repercussions they might inspire. Alas, they would not leave me in peace. Gentle as they were, there was tenacity to them, reminiscent of a dog that will not let go of your pants leg until given attention. My author-cuffs are tattered but having at last written, and now revised, this book, I hope to move about more freely.

For over three decades, I have worked with people suffering emotional, behavioral, and mental maladies. Together we have written poetry, performed dramatic enactments, and made music, but it is in painting and drawing with them that I feel most at home. In this book, I refer often to the visual arts experiences of clients, colleagues, and students. I embrace and appreciate many forms of the creative arts, but I am most comfortable in the visual realm.

In 1994 when the first edition of this book was published, it was in many ways a continuation of my first two books, *Existential Art Therapy: The Canvas Mirror* and *Essentials of Art Therapy Training and Practice.* In those earlier works, I laid out a philosophical foundation upon which all of my clinical and teaching efforts were built, and explored critical elements of our profession. Now, in 2007 as I revisit, update, and add to this text, I am aware that this second edition is influenced by all the subsequent writing I have done as well as by those of many other authors in our profession; trends in health care in the United States; professional licensure and credentialing issues; and new movements in art.

In a deeper sense, however, this second edition of *Introduction to Art Therapy: Faith in the Product* precedes all of my other written works. The content of this effort is the metaphorical ground from which the others have grown. The title of this book expresses my desire to explore prominent themes and dilemmas in our profession. Significant questions of the field are addressed but not necessarily answered. Instead, I offer positions that have evolved over the years in the hopes that my discussions will encourage readers to embrace the processes of reflection and questioning.

When this book was initially published, the inclusion of the word *faith* in the subtitle was an expression of my belief that the efficacy of art therapy could not be validated through quantifiable research methods. The intervening years have shown that this is not necessarily the case, and remarkable research efforts have been made that confirm the healing benefits of art-making (Kapitan, 1998; Kaplan, 2000; Belkofer, 2003). I suspect that there will be an ever-increasing number of scientific studies supporting the medicinal value of art. McNiff's (1998) vision of art-based research has also eased my misgivings regarding art therapy research processes. Nevertheless, I continue to think that the heart and soul of the work of art therapists is beyond the scope of precise measurement, and I remain convinced that the greatest validation of art therapy comes in the form of anecdotal testimony from clients. Such evidence is conveyed best in creative narratives that are primarily artistic expressions. I also adhere to the belief that to practice art therapy, one must have faith in healing qualities of art processes and products.

The subtitle also accentuates the role of the *product* in my ideas regarding the work of art therapists. For far too long, the products–art objects–created in art therapy sessions were relegated to a subordinate position beneath process in our literature. In this text, I make an effort to attend to that injustice.

Introduction to Art Therapy: Faith in the Product begins and ends with reference to love. These bookends provide the parameters of the work, both in the context of the writing process and context of clinical art therapy endeavors. Love is the source that first called us into the profession: love of art and love for people. Love sustains us as the work proceeds. I can think of nothing I'd rather have said of me when I am dead than that I lived my life in a loving manner.

When I wrote the first version of this text, I was a full-time art therapist working in a psychiatric hospital and a part-time art therapy educator. Now, I am a full-time educator and part-time clinician. Everything has changed, but ironically nothing's that different. When I was practicing in the hospital, I was intensely focused on clients' experiences and the things I learned from them. In those days, I was not concerned with academic issues related to literary form. One shift that will be evident to those who read the original and this second edition is that I have adopted the American Psychological Association format and cited other's works more appropriately this time to improve the scholarly quality of the book.

Another less evident shift is in the overall tone of the writing. As I look back at the original text, I sometimes wince at the stridency of the presentation. It seems I had an axe to grind then that I have since lost somewhere along the way. Either I've mellowed or grown wiser. Whichever the case, I am less convinced that my way is the right way. Rather, it is just my way, and to paraphrase the poet and theologian Rumi, there are countless ways to kiss the ground and many ways to practice art therapy.

In addition to the revisions of form that I have made to this book, I have included two new chapters. One offers brief summaries of a range of theoretical approaches to art therapy, and another introduces historical figures in the art therapy profession. These chapters evolved in response to feedback I've received from colleagues in art therapy education indicating their desire for a succinct, yet engaging, overview of these topics.

I hope that this book strikes you as a bit of a jigsaw puzzle. The work that art therapists do is mysterious, and it should neither be too easily described nor too readily understood. Should the reading become frustrating, I ask of you what I ask of clients: Trust me, have faith, and make some art. I hope the picture will be clearer when you have finished the book. Until then, I hope you will enjoy the reading and struggle with it.

BRUCE L. MOON
Milwaukee, Wisconsin

ACKNOWLEDGMENTS

I am in debt to many colleagues, teachers, and mentors who shaped my ideas about art therapy. Don Jones, ATR, HLM, laid the groundwork for my understanding of the healing power of art, and at varying stages of my career, he has served as my hero, supervisor, boss, collaborator, and friend. My approach to art therapy has been deeply influenced, both overtly and subtly, by many art therapy theorists. Among the most prominent of these are Pat Allen, Shaun McNiff, and Catherine Moon. Without these people, this book would not have been written.

I am grateful to many former students at the Harding Graduate Clinical Art Therapy Program, Marywood University, and Mount Mary College whose feedback helped shape this second edition. Their critical responses and constructive suggestions over a number of years were both insightful and encouraging.

I am also in debt to many clients with whom I have worked. Their emotional, behavioral, and artistic struggles have inspired and motivated me to write, and I hope this effort honors them.

I also want to express gratitude to Ling Olaes, an aspiring art therapist who edited the final work.

CONTENTS

ILLUSTRATIONS

INTRODUCTION TO ART THERAPY

Chapter 1

WHAT'S LOVE GOT TO DO WITH IT?

I often ask myself, why do I make art? As new students enter the graduate art therapy program at Mount Mary College, I ask them the same question, "Why do you make art?" Now I ask you, the reader, "Why do you make art?" Don't answer too quickly. I am not interested in the first answer that comes to mind. For art therapists, there is no more meaningful question to be asked; this question is a matter of philosophical bedrock. Our stability, our place in the therapy world, and our authenticity is anchored to our responses to this question.

How should I begin this book? Where should I start? Was this book's moment of conception some time on the morning of St. Patrick's Day 1967? Have the ensuing years been nothing less than an extended gestation period? Or did this book really begin to be written on an April afternoon in 1991 as I drove through a line of severe weather on my way to Macomb, Illinois, thinking only that I was going there to present a paper at an art therapy symposium? I had no inkling that my numb professional death walk was about to be exposed. Maybe this book began to be written when my mother died? I don't know. I don't know where to begin.

You know I've heard about people like me,
But I never made the connection,
We walk both sides of every street,
And find we've gone the wrong direction.

But there's no sense in looking back,
All roads lead to where we stand,
And I believe we'll walk them all,

3

No matter what we may have planned.
Don McLean, 1971

In 1967, I was a sophomore in high school in Sidney, Ohio. In those days, my life revolved around athletics and rock 'n' roll. I liked football and baseball, but lived and breathed basketball. On that particular morning of St. Patrick's Day, I was in gym class. We were being taught the basics of gymnastic apparatus, and I was attempting my first full flip off of the springboard. I didn't rotate completely and landed to the left of the safety mat, driving my left heel into the hardwood floor. The pain was instantaneous and blinding. I crushed my heel bone, ruptured my Achilles tendon, and essentially ended my participation in organized sports. For a few weeks after the injury, I was bedridden, and for the next 10 months, I was on crutches. I never again played on the basketball team, and my world view shattered. How could life revolve around that which was no longer possible? For the rest of my high school career, I was bothered by a slight limp, and since then, I have had to endure pain that comes and goes, and limitations that still remain (Figure 1).

Figure 1. *Gym Ghosts*–Acrylic on canvas.

I entered a deep adolescent malaise. Then my friend, Cliff (my first sort of art therapist), came to my rescue. Intuitively sensing the struggle I could not put into words, Cliff began to visit me at home after school. He had the reputation as the best artist at Sidney High School, and I was regarded as a solid guitarist. Cliff offered me a deal. "Bruce," he said, "I'll teach you to draw if you teach me to play guitar." I was desperate for company and consolation, and so our covenant was made. Every day after school, Cliff would come to my house, and for an hour or so, he would instruct me in the proper use of #2 lead pencils. For the second hour, I would teach him bar chords and lead riffs. In those dark hours of my young life, the arts brought me light, comfort, and meaning—and I survived (Figure 2).

Figure 2. *I Survived*–#2 pencil.

In the fall of 1990, Cain, an art therapist and faculty member of Western Illinois University, invited me to present an excerpt from my book *Existential Art Therapy: The Canvas Mirror* at a symposium that she was coordinating. As I drove I-70 across Ohio and Indiana, a line of tornadoes swirled just 20 miles south. It was quite a drive.

Over the previous two years, I had gradually assumed more and more administrative and supervisory responsibilities at the psychiatric hospital where I was working. In fact, my actual time with clients had been reduced to little more than one hour per day, and I had no studio art in my schedule at all. In place of clinical art therapy hours were program-planning meetings, budget meetings, supervision sessions, and a variety of committee meetings. The '90s were a difficult time for health care in the United States, and my non-client-contact days were filled with stress and conflict, both overt and covert. Against that backdrop, driving through tornadoes seemed like a perfectly normal thing to do. Looking back on that difficult period of my professional life, I think I had made myself numb so that I could just go through the motions.

Perhaps it was because I had no big expectations for the symposium. I was just going to present, try to relax, and enjoy myself. I was caught off guard when the keynote speaker, Whyte, began his address. With a deep resonating voice, he opened with this poem:

Waking

Get up from your bed
go out from your house,
follow the path you know so well,
so well that you see nothing
and hear nothing
unless something can cry loudly to you,
and for you it seems
even then
no cry is louder than yours
and in your own darkness
cries have gone unheard
as long as you can remember.

These are hard paths we tread
but they are green

and lined with leaf mould
and we must love their contours
as we love the body branching
with its veins and tunnels of dark earth.

I know that sometimes
your body is hard like a stone
on a path that storms break over,
embedded deeply
into that something that you think is you,
and you will not move
while the voice all around
tears the air
and fills the sky with jagged light.

But sometimes unawares
those sounds seem to descend
as if kneeling down into you
and you listen strangely caught
as the terrible voice moving closer
halts,
and in the silence now arriving
whispers

Get up, I depend
on you utterly.
Everything you need
you had
the moment before
you were born.
David Whyte, 1990, pp. 36–37

It is hard to describe, but the instant that he finished his recitation, something broke loose within me. I felt as if I'd been awakened from a long numbing sleep. On the 10-hour drive back to my home, I had two recurrent thoughts: I must paint, and I have to get out of the administrative world that has ensnared me.

Art, the common thread in these life stories, has caused me to think about the art therapy profession and what it means to be an art therapist. These experiences have made me question what drives our discipline. As part of my own life-review process, I have questioned my motivations, the inner push, and the energy that being an art therapist demands. How do we do it? How do we rise from our beds each morning and make our way to work, knowing that our hearts will be shattered as we watch a four-year-old boy scribble out the pain of his father's belt; knowing that our souls will be battered as we witness acrylic blood streaming down the canvas as a young woman portrays the nightmare that lives within her; and knowing that our sense of security will be tattered as a 70-year-old stroke victim offers images of what may wait for us in the future?

What is the source? How do adolescents survive life-altering injuries? How do administrators maintain their sanity amid insane health care systems? How do art therapists endure?

> *Everything you need*
> *you had*
> *the moment before*
> *you were born.*
>   David Whyte, 1990, p. 37

I believe that our source as art therapists is love. I feel a bit uneasy writing this because I know it sounds unsophisticated; still, this is what I believe. I have read graduate art therapy program catalogues from many colleges and universities, and I have scanned the tables of contents of many art therapy texts. I have reviewed the *Ethical Principles for Art Therapists,* and I've attended almost every American Art Therapy Association (AATA) national conference since 1975, but I have failed to find any direct mention of, or even veiled reference to, love. Yet I affirm that love is the force that motivates us art therapists to do the work that we do. I contend that it is love that first attracts students into the art therapy profession because making art is an act of love.

Of course, any attempt to explore this idea is an exercise in discussing things that are immeasurable, illogical, and mysterious. No scientific study will validate my assertions about the centrality of love in art therapy. No legislative body can mandate their truth or falsehood. No form of credentialing or certification testing can measure the reliability of this premise. Nevertheless, I think that an attempt must be made to grapple with this force for it is the foundation upon which many therapeutic structures are built. Making art is an act of love.

Throughout the history of the arts, innumerable paintings, poems, plays, songs, and dances have been created solely to describe or express love. If you listened to popular music on the radio for an hour, you probably would hear the word *love* hundreds of times. These modern day expressions range from the romantic to the raunchy, from the divine to the profane. But with few exceptions, historic works of art and current top 40 hits alike capture only partial facets of love.

Plato and the early Greek philosophers conceptualized three subcategories of love: *agape,* divine love; *philia,* strong attraction; and *eros,* erotic, sexual love. While this triadic tradition deserves intellectual respect, it will not suffice for the purposes in this text.

Pertaining to art therapy, I offer another definition of love: the will to attend to the self and to others. The inclusion of the word *will* signifies an explicit integration of intent and action. In my experience with activity-oriented therapy modalities, I subscribe to the adage that actions speak louder than words. That love is an *act* of will suggests that it is less an emotion or feeling, and more a manner of behaving. It is not enough to simply want to be loving or feel loved. Love must be expressed through actions toward others and oneself. *Will* also denotes that such actions are done out of free choice. To attend to another is an act of volition. We do not have to love, and we cannot be forced to love. However, we can choose to act out of love.

Implied in this definition, the will to attend to self and others is a quality of interactive reciprocity. I believe you cannot genuinely attend to another if you are not attentive to yourself. In the art therapy studio, this principle is enacted through the interactions of clients with their artworks; art therapists and their artworks; and clients and art therapists with one another. Being with the images and artworks of clients enhances my capacity to attend to my own creations. Likewise, familiarity with my artwork deepens my sensitivity to client imagery. The same is true of human interactions: The more comfortable I am with my interior world of demons and angels, the more comfortable I am in the company of clients' dragons and knights in shining armor. Through the reciprocal interaction of artworks and persons, a circular artistic process of loving is created.

Although loving is an act of will and choice, the force itself lacks goal and purpose. We love for the sake of loving. We attend to another for the sake of attending. We make art for the sake of making art. Such love does not increase in personal or professional power or prestige. Instead of material gain, it brings only itself, and that is the most mysterious aspect of love.

Clients come to therapy bearing their psychological scars, often remnants of physical, sexual, or emotional abuse. Persons who should have been safe supporters have often victimized the people who come to art therapists for help. Clients come hungry for attention, desperate for the soothing balm of love. Those who should have loved them have hurt them. Our clients long to be understood and held, and yet they are frightened, guarded, and defended from the curative effects of being loved.

The creation of art is an act of love. As the artist dips a brush into acrylics and moves pigment to an empty canvas, an image begins its journey from deep within to without. Lines form, shapes emerge, hues color, and an image is born. This is a process of attending to the soul, so subtle and profoundly moving that it resists verbal description. Only the artist can experience the full meaning of the unfolding event. The task of an art therapist is to attend, to serve as midwife to the birth of the artwork. This provides the client/artist with a restorative, healing milieu, which I define as love.

The artist establishes parameters of love through the performance of creative endeavors. The artist acts out of love during creation. The art therapist, through acceptance, praise, or confrontation, also acts out love by seriously engaging with and attending to the artwork and the client/artist. The mystery of this creative interaction among artist, image, and therapist is that such love is neither earned nor imposed. Creation and attending are acts of grace. They cannot be forced, and they are not deserved; they simply are.

The mystery is felt as the artist steps away from the canvas for a different perspective on the work. It is sensed as others pause in passing to absorb the meaning of the creation. The mystery is felt as the artist signs the work, knowing that the signature does more than denote, "I did this." Rather, it proclaims, "I am this!"

Being attended to sharpens one's ability to value self and others. Both the lover and the loved one see the world with new eyes. According to Frankl (1969), love does not make us blind; it lets us see. All actions and images are enhanced and given meaning through love. From meaning comes the motivation to create again. From creation comes meaning, which drives motivation and inspires more creations, and so on and so forth.

Fromm (1956) suggests that for love to exist, five human elements must be present: discipline, focus, patience, mastery, and faith. I believe that all of these must be present in the practice of art therapy because the relationship between art, art therapy, and love is tied to the presence of discipline, focus, patience, mastery, and faith.

Engaging in any art process requires discipline. We can never truly be good at anything if our efforts are undisciplined. This implies practice, repetition, and struggle. I have led art therapy supervision groups in which I ask participants to work with the same art piece over several months. Students and seasoned therapists alike often find this task difficult. They lament that it would be easier to work on several images rather than stay with the same one for an extended period. I typically redirect them to their work by saying: "There is always more that can be done. There is always a deeper level that the work can take you to." I do not take their struggles lightly, however. I know that it requires discipline to stick with the work, especially when it is not going well or when it seems like there's nothing left to do. Of course, I know that this is difficult. Still, my insistence that supervisees keep working with the same image sets the stage for all that follows.

Anything that we attempt to do, if we only do it when we are in the mood or feel like it, may be amusing; it may pass the time, but it will never be art. This presents difficulty in our culture, which has lost its aptitude for self-discipline. Compounding the problem, discipline must pervade the artist's entire existence; thus, it is not enough to apply order to isolated tasks like learning to paint. Discipline needs to be an ingrained attribute of the whole person.

Our culture deifies relaxation, time off, and time away from the rigors of disciplined, routine work. We have drifted toward being a society that lacks self-discipline. This deficiency can be seen in a host of sociological phenomena, including drug and alcohol abuse, domestic violence, dysfunctional families, and the divorce rate. Without self-discipline, life is random and chaotic, what Frankl (1969) describes as the "existential vacuum":

> The existential vacuum manifests itself mainly in a state of boredom. Now we can understand Schopenhauer when he said that mankind was apparently doomed to vacillate eternally between the two extremes of

distress and boredom. In actual fact, boredom is now causing, and certainly bringing to psychiatrists, more problems to solve than distress. (p. 129)

In the art therapy studios where I have worked, art therapists set the tone for disciplined engagement with the arts in many subtle ways. Perhaps easiest to describe is my approach to painting. I do not like to use pre-stretched, pre-gessoed, or factory-constructed canvases. From my first encounter with clients, I encourage an authentic and active engagement with materials and processes. I begin the therapeutic journey by teaching the client to use a miter saw to cut stretchers from 2 x 2s and construct the frame. Then I help them measure, cut, stretch, and staple their canvas. Applying gesso correctly is the final step in preparing to paint. This approach establishes a mode of authentic engagement with materials, tools, and procedures that become invaluable to clients as they struggle with creative expression. Additionally, this struggle is a metaphor for the intense self-discipline that clients may apply to the rigors of psychotherapy. If clients are to find or make meaning out of the chaos of life, it is critical that they exert control. Without discipline, there can be no art or love, and there will be no focus.

The ability to focus, what Fromm (1956) describes as *concentration,* is essential for true engagement in art. Anyone who has ever tried to learn to play the guitar, taken a ballet lesson, grappled with watercolors, or attempted to master digital video-editing techniques knows that concentration is critical. Yet, even more than discipline, focus is needed. So many things go on all at once. In a 20-minute drive to work, one can simultaneously listen to the radio, talk on a cell phone, eat an Egg McMuffin, and think about the day ahead and the ball game that will be on TV that night. Our culture might best be described as a monstrous, open-mouthed consumer. We have grown used to the visual stimulation popularized in the television series, "Miami Vice," in which no scene remained constant on the screen for more than a few seconds. This visual style was further refined by MTV and music videos. Political campaigns use fleeting visual images mixed with sound bytes to create impressions of candidates that offer little more than glimpses, slogans, and visual sensations.

To be still, without talking, listening, drinking, or doing something, is nearly impossible for many people. If there is no focus, there will be no art. In the art therapy studio, the art therapist monitors the atmosphere of the milieu to shape an atmosphere conducive to artistic focus. Sometimes therapist interventions are necessary to maintain a healthy, disciplined, and focused studio; however, the milieu should not be overly regimented or constrictive for that would impede spontaneity and creativity. An example of such monitoring is found in my work with adolescent clients in which one environmental element that often requires attention is the use of music.

Music is an integral cultural phenomenon for adolescents. At times, the stereo provides an invaluable point of connection between therapist and client. As McNiff (1989) notes, rock 'n' roll music has a primitive and powerful rhythm that stirs our inner creative forces. Music can set the tone for the studio in both positive and negative ways. Sometimes a song lyric or details of a musician's life provides the art therapist and client with a common place to initiate dialogue and establish a relationship. In other instances, adolescents may express resistance by turning the volume up so high that conversation is difficult, or by plugging themselves into an i-Pod and effectively isolating themselves from others in the studio. At other times, particular songs may be considered inappropriate for a treatment setting because of the violent or antisocial nature of their lyrics. Although I advocate freedom of expression, I still occasionally censor elements in the art therapy studio. As an art therapist, one of my crucial responsibilities is the maintenance of a safe and predictable therapeutic milieu. Music and other environmental elements can be health-promoting, or they can be detrimental to the overall tenor of the atmosphere.

There is no universally applicable recipe for maintaining a positive therapeutic milieu that promotes artistic focus, but art therapists should attend to all facets of the studio. Art therapists must continually assess whether or not the studio is safe, predictable, and devoted to art-making in the service of relationship-building. If the milieu is not safe, predictable, and artistically infectious, clients will find it hard to focus. If there is no focus, there can be no love or art.

Concentration requires patience. If you have ever tried to work with clay on a potter's wheel, you know that nothing is achieved without patience. Learning to throw on the wheel takes time and practice. It takes time to wedge clay properly to remove all of the air bubbles so that pieces will not explode during firing. It takes time to master the process of centering the clay on the wheel. When the clay is finally centered, one must patiently try, try, and try again to insert the thumbs properly to open the clay. It takes time to perfect pulling the clay upward. If one attempts to hurry or take shortcuts through any of these steps, the end result will be failure.

For many people, working patiently is as difficult as maintaining discipline and concentration. In western society, life fosters and rewards quick results. Nowhere is this phenomenon more apparent than in the popularity and use of laptop computers and PDAs. Research and calculations that would have taken hours to complete years ago are now made in fractions of seconds. GPS systems tell us were we are and how to get where we want to be, and Google is so popular that it is now an officially accepted verb in the English language. However, speed is not of the essence when it comes to art-making and love. In fact, doing things quickly may be the antithesis of doing them skillfully.

One of the most challenging tasks I have encountered in my work with clients is helping them slow down. Art processes provide a compelling action metaphor for this aspect of a client's treatment. Some aspects of artistic processes simply cannot be hurried. For example, raw canvas must be gessoed. Adolescent clients have often expressed frustration with this aspect of their work in the art therapy studio. I try never to miss these opportunities to comment on the nature of the arts, therapy, and life itself. I respond to the impatient client: "Well, you're going to have to let the gesso dry for the rest of this session. Why don't you use the time to think about what you are going to paint, or you might want to make some initial sketches to plan your painting."

Client: But I want to paint today.

Bruce: I understand, but some things just take time. You can't hurry this, or you'll make a mess of things.

Client: Can't I get started as soon as the gesso is mostly dry?

Bruce: No, you really have to wait until it's completely dry. That way, the canvas will be entirely sealed so it holds the paint better.

Client: But I really thought I'd get to start painting today. I don't want to think about it anymore, and I don't like to sketch. I want to paint.

Bruce: You know, I think the Rolling Stones (Jagger & Richards, 1969) said it best: "You can't always get what you want." Sometimes it is important to take your time and be patient.

Client: I don't like being patient. I want what I want when I want it.

Bruce: It doesn't work that way in art. You have to cooperate with the materials and procedures. That's sort of like life, you know!

Client: This is boring.

Bruce: Do you know where boredom comes from?

Client: What are you talking about?

Bruce: You said you are bored. I believe boredom comes from an absence of quality relationships. If you have good relationships in your life, no matter where you are or what you are doing, you are never bored. On the other hand, if you don't have quality relationships, you could be at Disney World and be bored. Do you see what I mean?

Client: What's that got to do with art?

Bruce: Good relationships take time to grow. You have to be patient with them, and they can't be hurried. It's the same with making art. You can't make the gesso dry any faster than it will. You have to be patient.

The goal of mastery is perhaps the most controversial for art therapists. Fromm (1956) asserts that the artist must be ultimately concerned with mastery of a task. If the art, therapy, and loving are not of concern, the novice can never really learn their intricacies. One may be a dabbler or hobbyist, but never the master of the art. When working with paint, for instance, I regard it as important that my students and clients learn to shade, dry-brush, layer, and wash. This way, they experience themselves as being capable of stopping, rethinking, and struggling with the painting process.

The element of mastery is contentious for art therapists because much of the literature of the profession argues that process is most important in the therapeutic use of art. In contrast, the products (finished artworks) that result from the therapeutic process receive significantly less attention in our literature. Because of this emphasis on process over product, the role of procedural mastery and aesthetic quality has been downplayed in art therapy. I am convinced that the tendency to accentuate process and overlook product has been unwise, and art therapy literature (Henley, 1992; C. H. Moon, 2002) has begun to address this issue. C. H. Moon's (2002) concept of "relational aesthetics" has been particularly helpful: She argues for an aesthetic characterized by "concern for the capacity of art to promote healthy interactions within and among people and the created world" (p. 140).

The tendency of art therapy literature to emphasize process over product represents, on one hand, the capacity of art that is made freely and without concern for aesthetic quality to express feelings and ideas that might be inhibited by formal artistic considerations. On the other hand, it may represent a fear about artistic competency. Historically, the art therapy community may have suffered from an unconscious product phobia, or perhaps this is the result of living in a culture that does not seem to value the arts processes or products. Regardless of the etiology of our hesitancy to address the artistic proficiency and aesthetic considerations that are implied in mastery, I believe this is essential to our profession.

The assertion that mastery and aesthetic sensibilities are essential to the art therapy profession has often stimulated heated discussion in workshops I have facilitated at conferences and academic settings throughout the United States. Those who complain about this contention argue that they do not consider themselves artists. I am never sure how to respond to these complaints. On one level, I do not understand why someone would enter the art therapy profession without feeling some measure of proficiency as an artist of some kind. Implicit in the decision to become an art therapist is a love for art processes and products. I also wonder if complaints about my position that art therapists must be artists and ought to manifest some form of mastery of media are born of misguided understandings of what it means to be an artist. My response to these complaints is always the same: "There is no magic that determines that one person is an artist and another is not. The only genuine route to mastery is practice."

My son Jesse has always loved basketball. Throughout his life, he has worked hard to become good at the game. He shoots well and has developed his skills in all aspects of the game. This is no accident; he has spent countless hours practicing. I will never forget when he tried out for the seventh grade basketball team and did not make the final roster. I was out of town the night that he was cut, and when I called home to see how the tryouts had gone, he cried on the phone. I ached for him. But by the time I got home two days later, he was back outside at our hoop practicing again, working toward next year's tryouts. Several years later, as a senior in high school, he was one of the captains of the team and, at the end of the season, was given the coach's most valuable player award. Jesse understands the nature of artistry, mastery, and practice.

In our culture, we have divided ideas about art. On one hand, we build elaborate multi-million dollar shrines (museums) to art. On the other hand, arts programs are often the first to be cut when school systems face budgetary problems. While some artworks are revered and deified, others are reviled and trivialized. An unfinished sketch by Picasso bears a high price tag, while a fully developed painting by an anonymous art student is auctioned off at a starving artist's sale for peanuts. Go figure.

What does it mean to be an artist? Can anyone be an artist? Artists are sometimes viewed as an exclusive club. This may be why so many of my clients have told me that they are not really artists. They have been told that the artist club is exclusive, and they do not belong. Even some art therapists I know have trouble calling themselves artists. There has been a sense of elitism in the art world that divides us into art producers and art consumers. When I was little, my mom never told me that she hoped I'd become an artist when I grew up. You just don't wish for things like that.

One of my earliest encounters with the therapeutic use of art came when I was young. My mother insisted that I go to church with her every Sunday morning. The pews were so hard, people sat so still, the sanctuary was always too hot, I hated my little bow tie, and the minister's sermons were unbearably long. As little boys do, I fidgeted and squirmed. My mother would hand me the church bulletin and whisper between clenched teeth, "Draw." So really, my mother introduced me to art therapy when I was three or four years old, and being an artist helped me survive the weekly torture of church.

Unfortunately, many people have lost touch with the ability to struggle. I have, for example, met some art therapists who lament that they cannot paint. I mourn the fact that they do not struggle with or practice painting. Rather, they give in to the frustration of failed efforts and avoid the pain of future disappointment by ceasing the activity. There are few things that are truly valuable in life that come conveniently. I encourage art therapists to reclaim their identity as artists who are ultimately concerned with both process and product in whatever media they choose to employ.

Each of these four elements, discipline, focus, patience, and mastery, depend upon faith. The practices of art, art therapy, and love demand faith. By this I mean that we must have faith in the goodness of life, the arts, others, and ourselves. Fromm (1956) suggests that only people who have faith in themselves are able to be faithful to and trustworthy of others. I would add that only art therapists who have faith in their own art processes and products are able to have faith in those of their clients. Without faith in the power of images and artworks to heal, we have no reason to be in the art therapy profession. This is why I am so disturbed when I hear colleagues bemoan the fact that they never make art for their own sake. They complain that there is just too little time, and that they are too busy, too tired, or too something else.

At every stage of my life, at least since St. Patrick's Day 1967, art has comforted me when I was in pain and afflicted me when I was too comfortable. Simple #2 lead pencil drawings helped me survive the life shattering injury to my left foot. The words of a poet awakened me from a numb administrative death walk, and when I returned from the symposium at Western Illinois University, I renegotiated my work schedule so that my clinical contact with clients was quadrupled. Not long after that, one of my paintings forecast my mother's death (B. L. Moon, 1992, pp. 159–163). That painting (Figure 3) prepared and strengthened me, as I became no one's son.

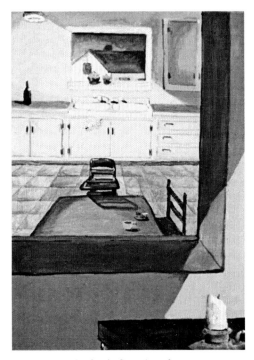

Figure 3. *No One's Son*–Acrylic on canvas.

Every little boy must have someone to look up to: a man who by his very being shows the boy what it means to be a man. In the best of situations, this initiation is done between fathers and sons. My father died when I was 18 months old. In his place, in my eyes, stepped my oldest sister's husband Marvin. As I grew up, Marvin was always important to me. He was big, strong, and fearless. Throughout most of my life, whenever I was in Marvin's presence, I felt special. I remember when I was young, he took me to a circus and put me on his shoulders because I was afraid of the elephants. I knew that no elephant could hurt me up there. I also remember him taking me to the train store and letting me pick out two accessories for my Lionel Train. He played football, built houses, and helped me build soapbox derby cars. Marvin took me fishing and taught me to hunt. One memorable afternoon in 1962, he explained how men and women make love. He was always there for me, doing things that fathers do.

In the time that I was growing up, Marvin built two houses for his family. I have vivid memories of these. The first one was constructed when I was four or five years old, but I remember carrying pieces of wood, sweeping up, and doing whatever I could to please him. I recall how badly his words stung as he nicknamed me "Lightning" because I wasn't moving as quickly as he wished.

By the time he was building the second house, I was a teenager. He gave me my first real paying summer job, helping him build that house. What a summer that was! I drank my first beer one hot July afternoon. The other men on the job told their off-color jokes as if I were just one of the guys, not just a kid anymore. Marvin was always larger than life to me.

In 1987, my wife Catherine and I built a house together. I nearly burst with pride when Marvin showed up on the first day of construction and praised the work I'd done on the main support beam. I have a photograph of him and me placing the last log at the peak of the roof (Figure 4). He was there as always.

Not long after we finished the house, Marvin was diagnosed with leukemia. Many medications were tried, but he continued to weaken. Blood transfusions helped, but the intervals between them continued to shrink. He faded, withered before my eyes, and finally died. We will build no more houses together. What can be done? How can I bear this life as it is? I must paint, and I must love.

Why do I make art? Why do you make art? I have no choice.

Figure 4. *The Last Log*–Photograph by Catherine Moon.

What's love got to do with it? Everything. I mean everything. Have faith (Figures 5 & 6).

Figure 5. *Building the House*–Acrylic on canvas.

Figure 6. *Building the House*–Acrylic on canvas.

Chapter 2

AN OVERVIEW OF ART THERAPY:
THEORIES AND HISTORY

Just as there is a multitude of media options available to art therapists, there are many theoretical orientations upon which to base our work. Rubin (1999) notes, "There have always been as many different approaches as there are art therapists" (p. 157). Art therapists tend to anchor their work in one or more of these theoretical frameworks. This chapter offers a short summary of the main schools of thought that have been incorporated into art therapy theory. It would be impossible in this context to fully describe the impact that these diverse theoretical orientations have had on various art therapy techniques. The purpose of this chapter is to provide an overview of the basic tenets of these schools of thought and summarize some of the ways that art therapy theorists have integrated these ideas into the practice art therapy.

The Art Psychotherapy–Art as Therapy Spectrum

In the broadest sense, the history of the art therapy discipline has been marked by a philosophic and theoretical spectrum between *art psychotherapy* and *art as therapy* approaches (Wadeson, Landgarten, McNiff, Free, & Levy, 1977). Lusebrink (1990) writes: "At one end of the art therapy spectrum is the use of visual media with focus on the product and artistic aspects. At the other end is emphasis on process, verbal free association to the images rendered and insight" (p. 10). In *Art Psychotherapy,* Wadeson (1980) states: "The field [art therapy] is a broad one with much variety among the approaches of different practitioners. Some place emphasis on the art, some on the therapy. . . .

Some art therapists consider themselves psychotherapists using art expression as a therapeutic modality" (p. xi). Between the two poles of the art therapy continuum are a number of theoretical subcategories.

Practitioners who use an art psychotherapy approach typically emphasize the process of expression and the client's verbalizations about the visual product. The development of psychological insight is the prime objective in this approach; thus, the artwork is seen as a means to an end with the end being verbal expression. Practitioners who use an art-as-therapy approach assert that the process of creating is itself therapeutic. According to Kramer (1971, 1993), the art therapist establishes the conditions for nurturance and support of the creative process by maintaining the studio space, and offering technical advice and emotional support. In this approach, the art therapist may serve as an artistic role model and teacher, and client verbalization and insight are not emphasized. In practice, most art therapists would describe their approach to clinical work as falling somewhere in between the art psychotherapy and art-as-therapy theoretical poles; of course, this may vary for a given therapist based on the specific client and site. Many art therapists would describe their style as a blend of several theoretical orientations. Despite the realities of pragmatic eclecticism, and for the sake of clarity in this overview of theoretical positions, I will discuss some of the most prominent art therapy theoretical approaches.

Art Psychotherapy Approaches

Throughout its history in the United States, art therapy has been rooted in two worlds: art and psychology. According to Vick (2003), "Art therapy is a hybrid discipline based primarily on the fields of art and psychology, drawing characteristics from each parent to evolve a unique new entity" (p. 5). The psychological root of art therapy grew out of psychoanalytic and psychodynamic theory. Rubin (1999) notes "Psychoanalysis is only one of many ways of trying to understand how and why people function as they do. But it is the oldest and most elaborate among modern therapeutic approaches, and has influenced all of the others, which are either modifications of or reactions to it" (p. 158).

Psychoanalytic Art Therapy

Freud is the most prominent of the early psychodynamic theoreticians. He is the father of psychoanalysis, and his therapeutic theories are based on understanding the powerful dynamics that shape the inner life of the client. Freud describes a model of the mind that includes three levels of consciousness, from the deepest and least accessible through the level of greatest awareness. These three levels of awareness are: unconscious, preconscious, and conscious. In addition, he postulates three divisions of the mind: the *id,* which comprises instinctual drives that are primarily sexual and aggressive; the *ego,* the negotiating aspect of the mind that attempts to find compromises between the impulses of the id and limitations of the *superego;* and the superego, a person's conscience or moral code.

Art therapists who work from a Freudian perspective generally view the impulse to make art as an expression of id energy. The approach used by Naumburg (1966), one of the earliest pioneers of art therapy in the United States, emphasizes the importance of free association in relation to spontaneous imagery to bring unconscious forces into conscious awareness and stimulate insight. Thus, Naumburg's approach was deeply indebted to Freud's psychoanalytic concepts. Kramer (1971/1993), another early art therapy theorist, emphasized the role of art-making in sublimation. Stated simply, sublimation is a process by which the ego transforms destructive energy into socially productive outcomes.

Art therapists working from a psychoanalytic perspective have two primary goals. First, they use spontaneous art processes and imagery to help clients free associate to uncover unconscious internalized conflicts that are the source of problems. Second, through the emotionally-charged transference relationship between client and therapist, they help clients understand the meaning of problematic behaviors in terms of previously unconscious dynamics. Both of these goals rely upon verbal interaction between client and therapist with art used to stimulate and focus therapeutic discussion.

Jung was a colleague of Freud who was influenced by psychoanalytic theories; however, Jung broke with Freud's teachings and founded analytical depth psychology. Jung hypothesizes that all people share a *collective unconscious,* and that certain universal archetypes are common to all cultures. In Jungian psychology, an archetype is an inherited memory represented in the mind by a universal symbol that can be observed in dreams and myths. Jung found support for his ideas in the similarities he observed in artistic traditions throughout the world.

Both Freudian and Jungian theories have been integrated into the practice of art therapy. Still, the theoretical rift between Freud and Jung that led to the development of separate approaches to therapy has also impacted art therapists. This can be seen in their divergent ideas about the functions of symbolism: Freud emphasizes the capacity of symbols to express the unconscious sexual and aggressive forces of the id in fantasies and feelings, whereas Jung accentuates the ability of symbols to unveil hidden ideas and universal truths. Thus, Freudian theorists tend to regard artistic imagery as a sort of psychological riddle and thereby approach imagery with a deductive perspective. Moon (1995) coined the term *imagicide* to describe that phenomenon. On one hand, art therapists working from this theoretical base are likely to view artworks as expressions of pathology. Jungian theorists, in contrast, tend to revere artistic imagery as both psychologically and culturally significant. Jung promotes using visual imagery along with movement and drama in a technique he calls *active imagination,* which is a creative way of intensifying and expressing ideas and feelings in therapy. Hence, Jungian art therapists are likely to encourage art activity as an expression of pathos.

Other strains of psychodynamic theory that have made their way into art therapy include Robbins' (1987, 2001) incorporation of object relations theory that stresses the role of art in containing and organizing phenomena; Lachman-Chapin's (1994) integration of self psychology; and Levick's (1983, 1986) emphasis on children's artworks as expressions of defense mechanisms.

Approaches Based in Humanism

In response to the emphasis that psychoanalytic theorists placed on clients' unseen dynamics, unconscious motivations, inner conflicts, and past experiences, another major branch of therapeutic approaches emerged under the umbrella of humanism. Humanism is a system of thought based on the values, characteristics, and behaviors believed to be best in human beings. Humanistic approaches to therapy are concerned with the needs, well-being, and interests of the individual client in the present. A hallmark of humanistic psychology is a model of change based in a wellness concept that sharply contrasts the medical model of pathology.

Maslow (1968, 1975), Rogers (1951, 1961), Adler (1958), Perls (1969), Frankl (1969), May (1975), Moustakas (1994), and Yalom (2005) are humanistic theorists who developed approaches to therapy that have been incorporated into art therapy practice. These theorists broke new ground by de-emphasizing the authority of the therapist and accentuating the inherent worth, dignity, and capacity for self-direction in clients.

Maslow (1968, 1975) developed transpersonal psychology, which deals with the best and highest potential in human nature. Transpersonal psychology emphasizes interpersonal connection, love, affection, and respect for others, and embraces the notion that longing for spiritual connection is essential to human development. Art therapists influenced by Maslow emphasize the capacity of art-making to foster psychological growth, self-actualization, and art activity as a form of spiritual contemplation and meditation. In transpersonal art therapy, artistic expression is seen as a way to explore not only the self, but also that which is beyond the self.

Art therapists who work from Rogers' (1951, 1961) person-centered approach use art processes to empower clients' capacities for growth and autonomy (Silverstone, 1997). To facilitate this, the art therapist strives to encounter the client with genuineness and authenticity; foster unconditional positive regard for the client; and develop an accurate empathic understanding of the client's subjective world. Rogerian art therapists endeavor to help clients realize that they have the capacity to help themselves. Art therapists encourage clients to express feelings without suggesting methods of change.

Adler, another colleague of Freud, began the individual psychology movement. His approach to therapy is notably integrated into the art therapy graduate education program at the Adler School of Professional Psychology in Chicago. Art therapists working from an Adlerian approach encourage clients to overcome feelings of insecurity and develop feelings of connectedness to others. The primary goals of Adlerian art therapy are to exchange clients' unrealistic needs for self-protection, self-enhancement, and self-indulgence with courageous social connectedness and social contribution.

Perls and his wife, Laura, developed gestalt therapy, an approach based on the premise that people must be understood in the context of their relationship with the world in which they live. "Gestalt therapy is lively and promotes direct experiencing rather than the abstractness of talking about situations" (Corey, 2005, p. 192). Rhyne (1973) integrates Perls' ideas into art therapy by emphasizing art experiences that focus clients' awareness and senses in the here-and-now. In addition to helping clients overcome dysfunctional symptoms, gestalt art therapists aim to enable clients to live more fully and creatively in the present. Clients are encouraged to experience their feelings and behaviors and perceive the self as a whole, a totality of many parts that together make up their reality.

Erickson's approach to strategic therapy with metaphoric communication and paradoxical interventions (as cited in Haley, 1973) has influenced the work of many art therapists (Jones, 1980; Mills & Crowley, 1986; B. L. Moon, 2007). Jones, an early American pioneer of art therapy, relies heavily on the magical power of metaphor to gently lead clients toward deeper understandings of their lives through guided imagery art experiences. In *The Role of Metaphor in Art Therapy: Theory, Method, and Experience,* I (B. L. Moon, 2007) identify seven advantages to using visual, aural, kinetic, and milieu metaphors in art therapy, including: (1) the stimulation that comes from visual artworks; (2) the less confrontational and psychologically threatening nature of indirect expressions over direct statements; (3) client access to conscious and unconscious meaning contained in metaphors; (4) chances for clients to reframe their experiences by looking at situations from new perspectives and making them concrete in visual images; (5) the introduction of artworks as a "third member" in therapeutic relationships; (6) building rapport between the art therapist and client through the acts of making and sharing; and (7) opportunities for art therapists to support, inform, engage, offer interpretations, provoke thought, and gently confront clients in safe, psychologically non-threatening ways.

Existential therapists (Frankl, 1969; May, 1975; Moustakas, 1994; Yalom, 1980) describe psychotherapy approaches based on the ultimate concerns of existence, believing that human beings have the ability to choose what they want to be. Ideas from these authors' writings were important influences in the development of principles for existential art therapy (B. L. Moon, 1990, 1995), which explores ways that art-making can support the creation of meaning in clients' lives. The primary tenets of existential art therapy are engagement in meaningful activity with the client; openness to being with the client regardless of what the client brings to the therapy; and honoring of a client's suffering.

Behavioral Art Therapy

Historically, art therapists have not embraced behavioral approaches to therapy. Rubin (1999) suggests that this is because "at first they appear antithetical to a genuine creative process" (p. 165). I believe that the reticence of art therapists to integrate behavioral theory may be because of the perception that behaviorists are not interested in the feelings and underlying motivations of the client; rather, they focus on the client's observable problematic behaviors. However, it is indisputable that making art is a behavior, and thus art therapy can be adapted to include behavioral therapy techniques. Behavioral art therapists use art activities to help clients deal with explicitly defined goals related to the client's current problems. The behavioral approach stresses a psycho-educational process through which clients learn self-management skills and self-control strategies. The practice of behavioral art therapy is grounded in a collaborative partnership between the client and art therapist, and conscious effort is made to inform clients about the nature of the treatment process. There is also an emphasis on practical application of the strategies for change that emerge in the therapeutic process (Corey, 2005).

Cognitive-Behavioral Art Therapy

Although many different strains of cognitive behavioral approaches to therapy exist, they tend to share the following characteristics: (1) a mutual and collaborative relationship between therapist and client; (2) a belief that psychological dysfunction results from disturbances in the thinking processes; (3) a focus on changing thoughts to change behavior and affect; and (4) time-limited therapy focused on specific problematic feelings or behaviors.

Ellis (1993) was an early champion of a cognitive approach to therapy. He developed rational-emotive behavior therapy, suggesting that life events are not necessarily responsible for negative emotions; rather a person's assumptions, expectations, and interpretations of life events are (Corey, 2005).

Cognitive-behavioral art therapists use art processes to help clients recognize false, destructive, and unhelpful beliefs and thoughts that negatively influence their behaviors and feelings. A cognitive-behavioral approach offers pragmatic and observable ways to reframe clients' negative patterns of behavior, which can be particularly helpful in short-term therapy.

Integrating Multiple Art Forms in Art Therapy

There is a significant body of literature advocating the use of all of the arts in art therapy. McNiff (1973, 1974, 1981, 1982, 1986, 1989, 1992, 1998, 2004) has long argued for integrating various art forms in what he describes as interpretive dialogue with images. "Art, like therapy, not only includes all of life but certainly the specific elements of gesture, body movement, imagery, sound, words, and enactment" (McNiff, 1982, p. 123).

Knill (2006), a long-time colleague of McNiff, advocates an intermodal expressive therapy approach that relies on the disciplined integration of all of the arts in therapy. Levine and Levine (1999) emphasize the capacity of individual imagination to integrate multiple dimensions of artistic activity and unify the array of experiences that can cause emotional disintegration.

A central tenet of a multi-modal, or integrative, arts approach is that when one responds to an artistic expression like painting through another artistic modality such as writing a poem, a transformative process of ever-intensifying expression is promoted whereby the client/artist comes to know the meanings of artworks more deeply. I (B. L. Moon, 1999, 2007) expand on these ideas in describing a process of responsive art-making through which the art therapist responds to clients' visual artworks through gestures, sounds, and poetry.

Feminist Art Therapy

Feminist art therapy places issues related to gender and power at the heart of the therapeutic process. C. H. Moon (2000) writes, "A feminist aesthetic paradigm of professionalism values such qualities as flexibility, creativity, inclusion, openness to interdisciplinary pursuits, being in relationship, engagement with ordinary life, emotionality, and artistic sensibilities" (p. 9). It is based on the principle that to understand the client, it is imperative to consider the social and cultural context that contributes to a client's difficulties. Corey (2005) says:

> A central concept in feminist therapy is the psychological oppression of women and the constraints imposed by the sociopolitical status to which women have been relegated. Our dominant culture reinforces submissive and self-sacrificing behaviors in women. The socialization of women inevitably affects their identity development, self-concept, goals and aspirations, and emotional well-being. (p. 341)

The AATA has a 94 percent female membership (Elkins, Stovall, & Malchiodi, 2003). "Given that art therapy is a profession dominated by women, there have been surprisingly few publications devoted to gender issues in art therapy" (Hogan, 1997, p. 11). Notable exceptions to the scarcity of feminist literature in art therapy are Hogan, 1997; Talbott-Green, 1989; and Cathy Moon, 2000 and 2002. In my opinion, it is also interesting to note that despite the prevalence of women in leadership positions within the AATA and the Art Therapy Credentials Board, both organizations have tended to operate from traditional male hierarchical models of leadership.

Postmodern Approaches to Art Therapy

Each of the theoretical orientations discussed so far have their own description of reality. In the past two decades, growing attention has been placed on the idea that many versions of reality exist simultaneously. This has led to skepticism that there is any one universal objective truth. "We have entered a postmodern world in which truth and reality are understood as points of view bounded by history and context rather than as objective, immutable facts" (Corey, 2005, p. 385).

Alter-Muri (1998) posits four assumptions on postmodern art therapy. First, dialogue is a shared reality between the therapist and the client, and language and visual images have powerful meaning. Second, meta-narratives, universal ideologies, and prescribed meanings for various symbols in artwork are not accepted. Third, every psychological theory and practice is specific to a culture and time in history; thus, therapists must always be aware of the multiple cultures that clients bring to a session, including family culture, religious culture, culture of origin, economic culture, and culture of the community and society. Finally, social action is the underlying goal.

In postmodern art therapy, images and art-making are viewed as ways to create meaning, and there may be as many versions of meaning as there are artworks that express them and artists who create them. Each of these image stories is true for the artist telling or creating the story, or both.

Narrative Approach to Art Therapy

The focus of narrative therapy involves the establishment of a collaborative relationship between therapist and client. The therapist's primary tasks in the relationship are: to intently listen to clients' stories to identify periods in clients' lives when they were good at problem-solving, especially in difficult situations; to interact with clients in a way that encourages self-exploration; to avoid labeling and diagnosing; to help clients chart the influence that a particular problem has had on their lives; and to help clients distance themselves from the prevailing stories they have internalized to make room for the creation of different and more satisfying life stories. In describing underlying assumptions of narrative therapy, Corey (2005) writes: "We live our lives by stories we tell about ourselves and that others tell about us. These stories actually shape reality in that they construct and constitute what we see, feel and do" (p. 397).

Riley (& Malchiodi, 1994; 1999) was instrumental in advancing the notion that art therapy is a social construction. She integrates narrative therapy understandings into her art therapy practice. "The art therapist offers media, the opportunity, and facilitates visual expression; the client chooses the focus, the subject, and the meaning of the art product" (p. 263). The notion that client-generated images and artworks represent meaningful expressions of the life stories of individual clients has been central to art therapy theory from its earliest days. What is new in the narrative therapy approach to art therapy however is the therapeutic perspective from which art therapists do not pathologize clients' images or offer static interpretations of clients' artworks. Perhaps most notable in the narrative therapy approach, art therapists do not prescribe particular artistic tasks or directives to avoid preset outcomes. Instead, clients are given freedom to tell their own stories through art-making and ascribe whatever meaning(s) they deem appropriate.

Eclectic Art Therapy

The term *eclectic* means made up of elements from various sources (Corey, 2005). Eclectic art therapists choose what they regard as the best approach from a range of sources or styles. Wadeson (as cited in Rubin, 2001) uses the metaphor of a layer cake to describe her integrated approach to art therapy as a blend of psychodynamic, humanistic, and behaviorist styles. One can argue that an eclectic approach allows art therapists the freedom to operate from any one of a number of theoretical orientations with a given client. On one hand, such an argument is appealing because it places clients' needs at the hub of therapeutic interaction. On the other hand, it can also be argued that eclecticism is a professional euphemism for a "jack-of-all-trades, master-of-none" approach. I believe an eclectic approach is most valid when enacted by seasoned practitioners with extensive experience operating from the various theoretical approaches that comprise their eclecticism.

Studio Art Therapy

The theoretical approaches to art therapy discussed to this point are derived from a school of thought originating in psychology. There are, however, more recent theories of art therapy that emanate directly from the artistic roots of the profession. The terms *art-based approach to art therapy, art as therapy,* and *studio art therapy* are often used interchangeably. Art-based art therapy theories place creative processes, various art forms, and artworks at the center of the theoretical construct. Art-based approaches to art therapy are "guided by the idea that art is a means to know the self" (Allen, 1995, p. xv). C. H. Moon (2002) further defines studio art therapy as:

> An intentional, disciplined, art-based art therapy practice. In such a practice, art remains central to all facets of the work, including: conceptual understandings; attempts to understand clients; creation of therapeutic space; development of treatment methods; interactions with clients; and communications that occur in relation to the work. (p. 22)

Interest in art-based approaches has risen steadily since the mid-1990s, and has served to rekindle discussion and debate regarding the role of art and place of artist's identity in the art therapy profession (Allen, 1992, 1995; Fleming, 1993; Lachman-Chapin, 1993; McNiff, 1995, 1998; B. L. Moon, 1994, 1995, 1998; C. H. Moon, 2002; Wix,

2000). The roles of art and artistic identity have been central philosophic questions since the early days of the AATA (Ault, 1977;
Wadeson, Landgarten, McNiff, Free, & Levy, 1977).

Spiritual Approaches to Art Therapy

In 1993, the theme of the national conference of the AATA was
Common Ground: The Arts, Therapy, Spirituality. The conference theme
signaled a growing acceptance of a significant but heretofore dissident
movement in art therapy thinking. Perhaps because of the influence of
Freudian psychodynamic theory in art therapy, which eschews spirituality as being non-rational, there was some resistance to dialogue
regarding this aspect of practice.

A central idea of spiritual approaches in art therapy is that art-making can be a form of spiritual practice. In a presentation at Ursuline
College, in Cleveland, Ohio, DeBrular (1988) discussed her view that
art processes are a mode of prayer. McNiff (1989) describes art as an
"unconscious religion" and art therapy as a modern expression of
shamanic traditions (pp. 20–24). McNiff (1989) and I (B. L. Moon,
1996, 2004) integrate Hillman's (1989) concept of soul as a perspective that changes random events into meaningful experiences through
understandings of creative process as a method of soul-making. A
number of authors have described art-making as a meditative practice
that leads to deeper connection with the self and others (Allen, 1995;
Horovitz-Darby, 1994; Horovitz, 1999; Franklin, Farelly-Hansen,
Marek, Swan-Foster, & Wallingford, 2000). C. H. Moon (2001) describes art practices in therapy contexts as expressions of prayer,
sacrament, and grace.

LOOKING IN THE REARVIEW MIRROR:
A BRIEF HISTORICAL OVERVIEW

We cannot set the course if we don't recall the past
the famous and the unknowns, I want to thank you now at last.
Thank you for the things you did, thank you for the things you said,
you ought to be in the books I've read
I thank the living, I thank the dead.

Bruce Moon, 2002, *The Acoustic Memory Project*

I remember sitting in a graduate seminar exploring the topic of *exegesis,* which refers to the process of explaining or interpreting a historical text or event. The professor warned our class that the exegetical process is dangerous and difficult. He admonished us to always be mindful of the hermeneutical perspective from which we viewed a particular text. "Hermeneutics is the inquiry concerned with the presuppositions and rules of the interpretation of some form of human expression, usually a written text, although it could also be an artistic expression of some kind" (Harvey, 1971, p. 117). The professor explained that, in his view, there are three essential qualities one must possess in order to accurately explain or interpret events or documents from the past: (1) a thorough knowledge of the historical context in which the events took place or the documents were produced; (2) a basic sympathy with the subject(s) of inquiry; and (3) a prior understanding of the fundamental issues with which the events or documents are concerned. Without these three elements, it is likely that events or documents, or both, may be misconstrued.

It is, then, with some trepidation that I attempt to provide a brief overview of the history of art therapy in the United States. While I believe that I have a fairly comprehensive knowledge of the historical context from which art therapy has grown over the past 70 years, and I am sympathetic with the subject and hold a fundamental understanding of the concerns of art therapy, I am also aware that I see the past through my own hermeneutical perspective. I know that my version of history has been influenced by the voices I have heard of significant figures in the profession, as well as by the absent silence of other voices.

In this context, I can only offer my interpretation of the history of art therapy. This is dangerous because my interpretation of our beginnings will likely overvalue or overlook one or more important events and persons. Still, as C. H. Moon (2002) states, "If a historical perspective is to be instructive, we must come to see ourselves as a continuation of the story being told" (p. 286). It is important to learn about the past so that we can more deeply understand how we have arrived at this place and time, and perhaps gain some sense of where we are heading.

The quasi-official history of art therapy in the United States has focused primarily on two overlapping groups of people: the so-called *pioneers* of art therapy and the *founders* of the AATA. Note that many art therapists who avoided the limelight were working at the same time as the celebrated pioneers and founders; although they are less known, they too were influential in the early development of the art therapy profession. It is particularly troubling, as C. H. Moon (2002) acknowledges, that "little has been written about the work of pioneering art therapists of color, such as African-American art therapists Lucille Venture, Georgette Powell, Sarah McGee, and Cliff Joseph" (p. 287). I am aware that as I am working on this second edition, there are contemporary art therapy authors committed to rectifying this deficiency in the literature of the profession.

The emergence of art therapy as an organized profession in the United States is generally Cane, Kramer, Huntoon, Jones, Kwiatkowska, and others, began documenting their work in various psychiatric or educational settings, or both. As Rubin (1999) notes:

> Not only are there many genetic roots; art therapy is a child with multiple parents, all with legitimate claims. In fact, as art therapy came to be better known, many individuals in different places appear to have given birth to remarkably similar ideas around the same time, often unknown to one another. (p. 101)

In 2002, I presented a performance artwork, *The Acoustic Memory Project,* at the national conference of the AATA. The performance was comprised of a series of interwoven monologues and songs intended to honor the early practitioners of art therapy. The following is a portion of one of the songs that addresses the difficulties inherent in attempting to depict the history of the art therapy profession:

> *It's Good to Paint*
>
> *Who's to say how this all began*
> *who defines the start*
> *The notion there is medicine*
> *hidden within art*
> *On the walls of the caverns*
> *buffalo were stained*
> *There must have been some voices*
> *sayin' yes, it's good to paint*
>
> *Plato spoke of images as*

medicine of soul
and the Navajo paint with sand
when evil spirits pull
Prinzhorn traveled everywhere
for the art of the insane
There must have been some voices
sayin' yes, it's good to paint

Some say this all began in the east
Some say it was the west
Some say it was out in Kansas
It doesn't really matter, I confess
Wherever you stand that's where you are
you know that old refrain
There must be some voices
sayin' yes, it's good to paint
                    Bruce Moon, 2002

When I envisioned the performance, I imagined writing six or seven songs that would recognize the influential characters of our history. I began my research by reviewing Rubin's (1999) accounts of the pioneers, and Junge and Asawa's (1994) history of art therapy in the United States. I also telephoned a number of the living founders of the AATA and asked them to tell me stories about the early days of art therapy. In no time, I had gathered a list of more than 40 names of art therapists or people who had supported the early development of art therapy, many of whom I had never heard.

The opening segment of the performance artwork began with a recitation of the following names: Gladys Agell, Charles Anderson, Rudolf Arnheim, Bob Ault, Florence Cane, Pedro Carones, Felice Cohen, Cay Drachnik, Paul Fink, Linda Gantt, Joe Garai, Gwen Gibson, Marge Howard, Mary Huntoon, Don Jones, Cliff Joseph, Sandra Kagin, Edith Kramer, Hanna Yaxa Kwiatkowska, Helen Landgarten, Myra Levick, Bernhard Levy, Viktor Lowenfeld, Vija Lusebrink, Sarah McGee, Micky McGraw, Shaun McNiff, Elsie Muller, Margaret Naumburg, Tarmo Pasto, Ben Ploger, Georgette Powell, Arthur Robbins, Janie Rhyne, Judy Rubin, Don Seiden, Bernie Stone, Prentiss Taylor, Don Uhlin, Elinor Ulman, Lucille Venture, and Harriett Wadeson. In-depth information regarding some of these individuals is readily available in art therapy literature or via the Internet. However, information is quite sparse on many of these people, and I have no doubt that other names should be on this list: people who labored in obscurity and were more interested in doing art therapy than writing about or presenting on it. I did not leave anyone off the list intentionally, and I hope that others will someday be able to tell the story of each of these groundbreakers.

For those interested in a more thorough discussion of the early development of art therapy, I would refer you to Rubin's (1999) and Vick's (2003) chapter on history, and Junge and Asawa's (1994) text. *Art Therapy: Journal of the American Art Therapy Association* and its predecessors, *American Journal of Art Therapy* and the *Bulletin of Art Therapy*, are also useful resources.

As important as it is to study the history and development of the art therapy profession, it is also important to be aware of our own hermeneutical perspective. The reality is that the ideas of art therapy are bigger than the identities of the American and European pioneers, and certainly broader than the particular thoughts associated with the founders of the AATA. As McNiff (2004) notes: "Art therapy is an idea and a profession that holds varieties as well as contradictions. It welcomes and assimilates the polarities of science, art, studio and clinic, artist and therapist" (p. 269). Whenever and wherever people have used imagination and creative process in the service of healing, the history of art therapy can be found.

Chapter 3

ARTIST OR THERAPIST

In 1975, I attended my first national conference of the AATA, and one of the presentations I attended addressed the question, am I an artist or a therapist? At the 1976 AATA conference, I listened to a panel presentation that focused on self-concept conflicts of art therapists (Wadeson, Landgarten, McNiff, Free, & Levy, 1977), as well as a paper by Ault (1977) that directly discussed the artist-or-therapist identity question. My initial response to these presentations, which at the time I kept to myself, was that these were odd questions. Up to this point, all of the art therapists I knew were active artists committed to their identity as such. With naiveté, I assumed that this was the case for every art therapist.

In the ensuing years, this artist-or-therapist identity question has often prompted spirited debate among art therapists. At some point, I have heard many first-generation members of our profession express their views on this question. Some of these art therapists say they focus their energy on cultivating their identity as therapists with a special affinity for using art processes in ways beneficial to their therapy work with clients (Feen-Calligan, & Sands-Goldstein, 1996). In contrast, my mentor, Jones (1980), adheres to the position that he is first and foremost an artist. His artistic authenticity is evidenced by his daily art practice throughout his career and further validated by his ongoing studio work since his retirement in 1988. As I write this in the spring of 2007, Jones continues to spend much of his time painting and sculpting—exactly what he always says is most important to him.

At the AATA conferences of 1975 and 1976, I kept my reactions to the aforementioned presentations to myself because I was, after all, a neophyte. Today, when students or colleagues ask whether I consider myself an artist or therapist, my response is always, "Yes."

Sometimes, the person who posed the question assumes that I misunderstood what was being asked and repeats, "Are you an artist first and foremost, or a therapist?"

Again, my answer is, "Yes."

If pressed to explain, I respond: "For me, art has always been therapeutic, and I am convinced that therapy is an art. How can I be anything other than both?" To separate or value one word of our professional title over the other hurts our professional identity.

Questions about the role of art in art therapy and importance of personal art practice for art therapists continue to be the subject of theoretical discourse in the art therapy professional community. In a provocative discussion that followed one recent panel presentation, a woman from the audience asked panel members to comment on her assertion that although she sees herself as a competent art therapist, she does not consider herself to be an artist or desire to become one. The woman's response to the panel was interesting and made me wonder what had motivated her to enter the art therapy profession in the first place.

Questions about art therapists' professional identity continue to be asked and, in fact, have been expanded upon. At a recent national conference of the AATA, there was much attention and discussion on the variety of roles that contemporary art therapists play in their work settings, including artist, clinician, assessor, educator, healer, art teacher, individual therapist, group leader, case manager, administrator, shaman, social activist, community-builder, researcher, and supervisor. Regardless of the many functions art therapists may serve, I believe that art therapists should be both active and practicing artists, and well-informed and committed therapists; these roles must not be separated. Although semantically unusual, and perhaps grammatically awkward, it would be helpful to our professional identity to describe ourselves as *arttherapists*.

For over three decades, I have participated in conferences and symposia where questions related to our profession have been discussed. Recently, in talking about this ongoing identity question in a class session, one of the graduate students at Mount Mary College asked, "Don't you ever get tired of talking about this artist or therapist question?"

I responded: "No, I think this is a critical and essential question because it addresses the soul of the discipline. It deals with where we art therapists came from, and I believe our answer to that question defines who we are, both as individual art therapists and as a professional community. So, in a sense, wrestling with such questions is a sign of dynamic life in the profession, and I never get tired of that."

As discussed in the second chapter, it is difficult to pinpoint where, when, and by whom art as therapy was first used. Some would argue that our roots go back to the ancient cave paintings of Lascaux, France. Others point to early writings by Freud that mention the imagery of his clients. Certainly Jung was a significant figure who valued the role of the arts, both in his own life and in his work with clients. Still others credit Prinzhorn for bringing attention to the art of the insane, thus stirring interest in the formal use of the arts as therapeutic agents. In this country, "pioneers" of the profession seem to have spontaneously begun the occupation in the mid-1900s. However, art therapy originated, there is a consistently high regard for images, art processes, and products. This leads me to believe that we art therapists should view ourselves equally as artists and therapists: *arttherapists*. It is a fascinating conundrum that art materials, processes, products, and history have so far received relatively little attention in art therapy literature and academe.

The educational journey of art therapy graduate students is complex, traveling many paths simultaneously. One path is filled with books, articles, and lectures. Another is littered with powerful emotional experiences unlike anything most students have experienced before. There is yet another path: an inward one defined by images in students' artworks as they brave the educational process.

I'm not sure why so little attention has been given to the art aspects of our collective persona. In my role as the director of a graduate art therapy program, I often hear students complain that they have no time to paint or draw because of the demands of schoolwork. Art therapy colleagues who say their jobs make it impossible to make their own art echo these complaints. I counter these lamentations by saying, one always has time for what is really important. When my children were younger and living at home, I made time to hug my daughter and play basketball with my son, and I was never too busy to kiss my wife. Likewise, I make time to make art.

The role of personal art-making for art therapists is more than a matter of semantic interest; it is a matter of professional survival.

Presently, many disciplines in health-related fields are facing difficulties. I have known many social workers, activity therapists, and art therapists who have chosen or been forced to leave their fields due to the unfavorable financial climate of health care in America. Psychologists lament that they are relegated to providing assessment services rather than treatment. Psychiatrists bemoan that because of managed care, they are only allowed to prescribe medications, not really provide the full range of services for which they were trained. I have heard art therapy colleagues wonder aloud if they made the right decision when they chose the field of art therapy as their life's work.

I can, in good conscience, say that I have never had such misgivings about my vocational decision. Of course, I am not immune to the insecurities about future employment that plague everyone in uncertain times. Still, this does not alter my resolve to be an art therapist. I feel secure at my foundation: the art. I know that to make art is good, and I have faith in the products and processes of art-making. My anchor in the turbulent worlds of health care and academia is my own art practice. The images that come to me as a result of my contacts with clients and their artworks deepen and enrich my life. The only times I have felt the numbness of burnout have been when I strayed too far or for too long away from my studio. I know that in an existential sense, I could live without being an art therapist, but I do not think I could survive psychologically without making art.

When students ask me for guidance on their prospects for future employment, I respond to their questions in the most authentic manner I can: "If you stay active as an artist, you will survive in this profession. If you give up making art for your own sake, you may in all likelihood leave the field if things become too difficult."

An artist is one who professes and practices an imaginative art. This definition does not mandate exhibitions or enter juried competitions; rather it leads to a definition of the art therapist as one who practices an imaginative art and attends to others through the processes and products of artistic work. Art is the anchor, the heart and soul, and one of the taproots of the profession.

Since the taproots of art therapy are art and psychology, one may wonder why there has been such long-standing debate about professional identity. The roots of this division are traceable to the haughtiness of some persons who describe themselves as artists and pomposity of others who carry the title of therapist. Perhaps it is human nature, but both artists and therapists have an ample quantity of vocational snobbery. I have been fortunate to function in the separate realms of each. For nearly 13 years, I taught at a professional arts school, the Columbus College of Art and Design. In that setting, I was often confronted with the vain glory of faculty members and students. In this culture, a hierarchical pyramid placed fine arts practitioners at the top, commercial artists at the bottom, and illustrators and fashion designers somewhere in between. The fine arts people behaved as though they were the only true artists in the school, whereas the commercial artists smirked that the "fine artsies" would have a rude awakening when they went out into the real world and tried to make a living being creative and self-expressive. The hostility between these factions was usually subtle, yet never far from the surface. The tragedy of this caste system was that the various subgroups missed opportunities to learn from one another. Occasions that could have enriched their learning were often avoided because of fear of contamination and ego wars.

In my role at the college, I often sensed mistrust from my art colleagues. In a faculty meeting, one of my peers told me that other faculty members were leery of art therapy because art therapists ascribe meanings to, or make interpretations of, artworks that go beyond commenting on media and technique. I had no way to confirm my peer's statement, yet I suspect there was at least a grain of truth in his words. In *Existential Art Therapy: The Canvas Mirror,* I (B. L. Moon, 1995) assert, "Artists have always known that a major source of their creativity is their own inner emotional turmoil" (p. 86). It is understandable, then, that people in the art community would be reticent to fraternize with art therapists in fear that art therapists would intrusively or secretly analyze or interpret their artworks.

I also have had extensive experience interacting in psychiatric institutions and psychological treatment communities. In these spheres, there are also hierarchical pyramids; however, they tend to be clad in professional civility. In such systems, the psychiatry profession sits atop the pyramid of institutional power and prestige, with psychoanalysis hovering just above the pinnacle. Psychologists, who are considered higher in rank than counselors and social workers, are just beneath psychiatry. Sometimes, there is a layer of creative arts therapists, nurses, adjunctive therapists, chaplains, and other technical specialists. Psychiatric aids and attendants are at the base of the pyramid.

Members of each stratum are typically rewarded commensurate with their station in the system. I have always found it fascinating that this system works in such a way as to inadvertently discourage contact with clients. By this I mean that those persons at the lowest level of the pyramid, the aids and attendants, spend the most time with clients, yet are paid the smallest amount and have the least power in the institution. On the other hand, psychiatrists typically spend the least amount of time with clients, but are reimbursed the most for their efforts and have the most institutional influence. It is interesting to note that Freud's psychoanalytic model of therapy was better understood and applied by writers and artists than by doctors (Papini, 1934).

Perhaps at some deep level, there is awareness on the part of the medical professional community that artists, not doctors, are the prototype analysts. This would explain why, in some treatment settings, art therapists are regarded with a measure of discomfort. Perhaps it is art therapists' comfort in dealing with clients' deeply disturbing imagery that inspires a veiled disciplinary rivalry that is publicly unacceptable.

Arrogance and competition in professional communities is expressed in many ways. Foremost among such expressions is the belief that members of one discipline know how to do therapy more skillfully, more effectively, or more efficiently than members of another discipline. Historically, psychiatry expressed such biases against psychology. Psychology in turn expressed biases against counseling and social work. This also happens within different segments of an institution, as well as between competing centers of care. For instance, I consulted for the activity therapy department in a psychiatric hospital for a period of six months. In this facility, the adolescent division of the hospital was convinced that the adult division didn't know how to treat clients correctly. The adult division felt that members of the adolescent division were overly controlling and heavy-handed in their approach to treatment. This rivalry negatively affected the members of the activity therapy department who felt they had to choose sides. At the same time, members of both divisions vociferously declared that their institution's standards of care were far superior to those of a competing hospital across town.

The art therapy professional community has inherited a tradition of hubris from both of our ancestral disciplinary roots: art and therapy. Unfortunately, this tradition is maintained as students come into the field from different directions. I suggest that we appeal to the higher natures of our lineage. Artists have always had a unique creative capacity to integrate polarities in their work. The creative act of making art is an alchemical process, transforming powerful conflicting forces within the artist (B. L. Moon, 1990, 1995). Through creative transformative actions, we may be able to forge a collective identity inclusive of all the disparate influences that contribute to our professional identity.

The Greek root of the word therapy means *to be attentive to.* Surely this implies the ability to attend respectfully to our differences and commonalities in service. Art therapy is more than the actions of sensitive humanitarian artists, and more meaningful than the techniques of verbal psychotherapists who experiment with crayons and markers in their work with clients. It is the marvelous covenantal relationship of art and therapy that fuels the powerful work we do. Each aspect of our professional identity embellishes and enhances the other, and the absence of either diminishes both.

When I am asked, are you an artist or a therapist, my response is always the same, "Yes!" I hope that this will be your answer as well.

Chapter 4

ART PROCESS AND PRODUCT

In an early document describing the psychotherapeutic use of art, Jones (1974) suggests: "Emphasis must be placed on the process not the product. A simple stick figure may be more meaningful than an elaborate painting." This view of the components of therapeutic artwork went unchallenged for many years as the art therapy profession developed in the United States. Evidence of the continued prevalence of this position is seen annually at national conferences of the AATA. Reproductions of clients' art products are often presented in slides or PowerPoint presentations of poor quality. The artworks tend to be rough and aesthetically challenged. At the same time, art therapists' discussions of clients' artworks typically focus on pathology, indicators of personality deviance, and interpretive intrigue.

Bias about the value of process over product can be seen in abstracts prepared for the AATA conference proceedings. Seldom have the topics of the aesthetics of the client/artist or the art therapist as artist been addressed. There have been exceptions to this, but by and large, the professional gatherings of art therapists have been devoid of reference to the quality of art by the client or therapist. Jones, to the best of my knowledge, first introduced slides of his own paintings in a presentation at the AATA conference several years ago.

More recently art therapists have stepped to the forefront of this issue by publicly displaying their products as artists in presentations, publications, and exhibitions of their work. In *Existential Art Therapy: The Canvas Mirror* (1990, 1995), I posit that art therapists must remain artistically active to stay honest in our profession. If not, they risk the damage that artistic inactivity does to the authenticity of art therapists. In that book, I included a discussion of 17 of my paintings as a plea for artists/therapists to return to their studios.

I am not alone in this hope. In 1989, art therapists DeBrular and C. H. Moon staged a two-woman show of paintings, sculptures, and quilts in the exhibit hall of the Methodist Theological School in Ohio. Their focus was not on artwork done by art therapists but, rather, works created by two women artists. Soon thereafter, McNiff (1992) devoted the last 81 pages of his text to exploring the messages of a number of his paintings. A meta-message of this segment of the book is that McNiff is confident in his proficiency as an artist and willing to withstand the potential criticism that the inclusion of his products may engender. Also in 1992, Allen described a model for art therapists that she terms *the artist in residence.* She proposed that art therapists reclaim their tradition as artists and avoid the complications of becoming overly clinified. Each of these examples, and many unmentioned ones, point to a growing movement in the art therapy profession that reclaims the role of the artist as a crucial aspect of our professional personality.

It was puzzling that such a movement should be necessary at all in a profession in which the first word of its name is *art.* I suspect that the art appellation lost its significance as the profession moved to define itself in the company of psychiatry, psychology, and social work. Perhaps unintentionally, as early leaders of the discipline struggled for professional recognition and prestige, efforts were made to master the language of these other more established occupations. It was as if art therapists longed to be seen as equals to physicians, psychologists, and family therapists. Although it is easy to understand the motivations of those in the forefront of such efforts as the field of art therapy developed, it is also easy to see in retrospect that much of our unique identity as artists/therapists was abandoned along the way. The motives for being like psychiatry or psychology are apparent: increased earning potential, potential administrative influence, employability, and professional prestige. All of these were powerful persuaders that lured the art therapy profession away from its roots in the art world. What emerged was a generation of art therapists fluent in statistical study, psychological jargon, and political savvy, but insecure about the integral place of the arts in the treatment of human suffering.

Despite encouraging signs about the resurgence of the role of aesthetics in the professional life of the art therapist, the field is still divided on this issue. Many in the profession continue to insist that art therapy must imitate other health care disciplines. This is evidenced in the guidelines for approval of master's level academic programs, and national trends toward licensure as counselors, marriage and family therapists, and other helping disciplines.

The power and depth of artistic expression demands that we art therapists be sensitive to nuances of color and shade, the push and pull of emotional currents that take course through line character, and the aesthetic sensibilities inherent in the balancing of weight and mass. Those who become art therapists should resist temptations to aspire to the lifestyle of the physician or the institutional political power of the psychologist. Students of the field should instead insist that they be trained as art therapists and nothing less than that.

The art therapy profession is connected to the sensual. The core of our work revolves around the senses: taste, touch, sight, smell, and sound. This establishes an inherent tension between art therapists and members of other verbally oriented disciplines because our primary therapeutic language cannot be found in a dictionary. Our language is found in studios, exhibitions, and museums. Art therapists ought to be cautious about movements that lead us to become pseudo-counselors. We must always keep in touch with our disciplinary heritage in the arts.

The Anguish of Aaron

Aaron came to my private practice office complaining that he was "always depressed and worried." A pleasant and gentle man in his mid-30s, Aaron had been treated for alcoholism at a residential center for several weeks the year prior. In our intake session, he told me he had remained sober for 13 months, and that although he felt positively about not drinking, he simply could not shake the feelings of emptiness and pointlessness that plagued him. Aaron told me that he was in his second year of graduate school and that he was going to complete his master's in business administration in the spring. He was unmarried and "on the rebound" from an intense relationship with a woman he had planned to marry. She left him for another man.

I asked Aaron what he hoped to get out of coming to see me.

"I am not sure," he answered. "A friend suggested that I try art therapy, and I got your name from the hospital. I feel like I've tried a lot of other stuff, so why not this?"

I asked again, "What do you hope for from our relationship?"

He sat quietly then said: "I guess I want to get control of myself. I want to feel better."

I handed him a large pad of newsprint and a box of pastel chalks. "Aaron, I'm not sure that I am the best person for you to see for therapy," I said. "It would help me if you would draw a portrait of how you feel."

Looking surprised, he asked: "What do you mean you aren't sure? Why?"

"Well, this practice is small, and I can only work with a few clients at a time," I said. "I have to be sure that you really want to do the work that you say you want to do. Now, would you please start your drawing?"

Although he looked as if he had more questions, he began to work. Aaron drew a circle, about two inches in diameter in the lower right side of the page. Then, using black chalk, he covered the rest of the sheet of newsprint. In the middle of the circle, he scribbled an intense red asterisk. In less than five minutes, he handed the pad back to me and said that he was finished. The design was visually interesting but his handling of the media was slipshod. Because of his careless application of the chalk, the image seemed messy, impulsive, and incoherent.

Without commenting on the drawing, I asked Aaron how his grades were and if he liked graduate school. Although he clearly liked the idea of having a master's degree, his answers hinted that he was doing just enough to get by and that he did not particularly enjoy his studies. He then initiated a long story of how he had begun to drink in his early teens. He essentially recited the work that he had done in completing the first step of Alcoholics Anonymous.

I asked, "Were you good at drinking?"

He looked at me incredulously and said, "What kind of a question is that?"

"Were you good at drinking?" I asked again.

Aaron's face reddened. "Well, I guess so," he said. "But what does that have to do with anything?" He sounded irritated.

I placed his drawing on the floor between our two chairs and said: "You seem to want to hurry through things like your drawing, Aaron. I didn't put any time limits on how long you could work. The task was to draw a portrait of how you've been feeling. By your own account, you've been feeling sad and empty for a long time; it was surprising to me that you could draw such profound feelings so quickly."

"I don't get this!" he exclaimed.

I said, "Aaron, I wanted to know if you were good at drinking because I am interested in things that you really have paid attention to and taken your time on in your life."

"I don't see what in the hell this has to do with anything," he said.

I replied, "Aaron, I am willing to see you in therapy on one condition: You commit yourself to working diligently with art."

"Why?" he asked.

"I think that you already know a lot about your feelings, but you don't seem to think much of yourself," I said. "What I have to offer you, as an art therapist, is my willingness to help you work with the images inside you. I believe that they have things to teach you, but you have to handle them with care and respect. That means taking your time and attending to them."

Aaron looked down at his drawing and said: "I don't want to sound rude, Mr. Moon, but it almost seems like you care more about my picture than me. I think maybe I've made a mistake. I don't think you'll be able to help me."

"You are probably right, Aaron," I said. "If you don't believe that I can be of help then I certainly won't be. It's your choice. Why don't you think about it and give me a call if you want to start. If I don't hear from you in a couple of weeks, I'll assume that you have decided against working with me."

As Aaron left the office that afternoon, he took his drawing with him; still, I suspected that I would not hear from him again. Nearly six months had passed when he called to set up another appointment. He asked, "When would be a good time for me to come to your office?"

I responded, "Do you really want to work with me in art therapy?"

"Yes, that's why I called you," he said.

"Then meet me at the studio at 7:00 Thursday night," I said.

He immediately began to ask why we would not be getting together at the office, what we would be doing, and how he should dress. I told him that I wanted to teach him to paint and that he should come wearing clothes that he wouldn't mind getting dirty.

Aaron arrived at the studio promptly. He looked around for a minute or two, taking in the paintings on the walls and the sculptures cluttering the benches, artifacts of clients past and present.

Enthusiastically, he said, "What am I going to paint first?"

"I don't know," I replied. "All that we are going to do tonight is build the canvas."

With slightly less eagerness, he said, "So, where do we start?"

I pulled two 2 x 2s from the wood rack and said: "Since this is your first painting, let's start small. I'd like you to measure two pieces 24 inches long, and two pieces 28 inches long." I handed him a tape measure and carpenters pencil.

When he finished marking the wood, he asked, "Now what?"

I gestured toward the hand miter box and said, "Set the angle for 45 degrees and cut each end of your 2 x 2s." I was operating on a hunch that Aaron had not had many experiences in his life with hand tools or building processes. Likewise, I suspected that he had not experienced parallel play/work situations with his father. It was my belief that he was hungry for positive encounters with an accepting male who would do things with him.

I watched as he approached the miter box tentatively. He clearly did not know where to position the 2 x 2, or how to place his hands so that he could both operate the saw and clamp the piece of wood to the metal back wall of the miter box. He also seemed unsure of how to adjust the angle mechanism of the saw. Without commenting on his lack of knowledge about the saw and box, I showed Aaron how to change the angle and position the wood. I left the sawing to him. He began to pull the saw hesitantly. "It won't bite," I said.

Without stopping, he replied, "I've never done this before."

"You are doing just fine, Aaron," I said.

When all his cuts were made, I gave him a piece of coarse sandpaper and suggested that he smooth the edges that he'd just cut.

"Why, they aren't going to show, are they?" he asked.

"No, they won't show, but they will fit together more snugly," I said. "You'll feel better about the joints if they are clean and tight. There is no substitute for quality."

"This is taking longer than I thought," he said with a sigh. "I thought I'd be painting something tonight."

As I continued to work on the stretcher frame that I was building, I said: "Aaron, you have got to learn the five Ps: Patience and Planning Provide for Positive Performance. Building stretchers is all about patience."

"But couldn't I just go to the store and buy a canvas that is already stretched and painted white?" he asked.

"Sure you could," I said, "but you can't do that and work with me." He asked why, and I said: "Because if you buy a pre-stretched, pre-gessoed canvas, you've already cut yourself off from the process. You miss an opportunity to be in touch with the soul of the painting."

When each of the angled cuts had been sanded, I showed Aaron how to clamp two pieces together to nail them securely. After he put the last nail in, he held up the rectangular frame for inspection. It was clearly a moment of gratification and pride for him. "Does the canvas go on now?"

"No," I said. "First we need to use the carpenters square to check all of the corners, then we'll make a couple angle braces to make sure that the frame doesn't distort when we stretch the canvas." By the time we finished, Aaron's hour was nearly over. "Aaron, we should discuss the financial arrangements for your therapy," I said. "There are a couple of options."

"Oh yeah, I almost forgot about that part," he said.

I replied: "If you would like to use your medical insurance, the fee will be $60 per session. I'll expect you to pay $30 at the end of each session. The rest you can pay me when you get reimbursed by the insurance company."

"I think I'd like to avoid the insurance company," he said. "If I use them, I'll have to talk with my employer again. That got a little embarrassing last year. How does payment work if I don't use insurance?"

"I work on a sliding scale, so it depends on how much you earn," I said. "For instance, if you make $30,000 a year, I charge $30 per session. If you make $50,000, it will be $50. The most I charge anybody is $70, and the least I charge is $25. So, you tell me how much you owe me."

Aaron wrote a check for $45. He said: "You talk about the bill very nicely. One of my other counselors always hemmed and hawed about money. He seemed embarrassed."

"I don't mind talking about the fee at all," I said. "I believe in the product you are purchasing, and I know that I will give you the best quality service at my disposal."

In a variety of ways, this session set the tone for the rest of the time I spent with Aaron. Our interactions most often focused on the tasks at hand: stretching canvas, planning paintings and technical details, and framing and setting hanging wire on the back. From gathering tools and materials to signing and displaying the finished product, each step was done with care and concern for quality. Note that Aaron did not come to me with a sense of himself as an adequate artist; in fact, the opposite is nearer to the truth. He came bearing his emptiness and self-loathing. It was critical that I engage him at the level he desperately longed for and help him develop a more positive regard for himself through doing. Mastery of task, coupled with self-expression, was the treatment of choice for Aaron.

Bly (1990) points out that prior to the industrial revolution, young boys spent time with their fathers who plowed the fields, worked in shops, or built houses. This provided boys with experiences that taught them what it meant to be a man, thereby initiating them into manhood. However, in the modern era, few such opportunities exist between fathers and sons. This leaves the son with an empty hunger for masculine relationships (Figure 7).

Figure 7. *This Leaves the Son with an Empty Hunger*–Chalk on paper.

The therapy for Aaron became a process of doing things together and investing attention in the quality of the work. By making things together, Aaron got to experience the healing effects of being in the company of an older male who did not judge or abandon him, and the therapeutic effect of the expressive arts processes. He also developed a more positive view of himself as he worked with and gained mastery over materials and procedures.

The third painting that Aaron worked on illustrates the relationship between mastery of materials and self-image. It was a large work, approximately 3' x 4'. The scene was of a stark white house, bathed in bluish-green light from a street lamp. The night sky was very dark, and a woman stood in the open doorway, dressed in a red half-open robe. She appeared to be looking for something or someone in the darkness. The painting seemed cold, yet it had a quality of passion and expectancy. The first time I saw it, the sky was painted a dull black, and appeared flat and empty. "Aaron, do you want the sky to look dead?" I asked.

He shook his head. "No, but I want it to be really dark," he said. "I tried to mix up a midnight blue, but I couldn't get it the way I wanted, so I gave up."

I studied the painting and said: "Well, I think we ought to back up and make a dark blue for the sky. It really needs more depth than the flat black can give."

"But I've already painted the sky," he said. "Do you know how much paint it took to cover all that canvas?" He raised his voice. "Do you know how long it took to paint it black?"

"It doesn't matter how long or how much paint it took, Aaron," I said. "It doesn't look right. There is no substitute for quality work. What colors did you use to try to mix midnight blue?"

He told me he had blended cobalt blue with warm black.

"Oh," I said. "That was the problem. Let's try it again, only this time, try using ultramarine blue as the base."

Aaron sighed and said: "I really think that this is a waste of time and money. I already used a lot of black."

I replied: "I'll be glad to help you, Aaron. But I won't do it for you. You know this reminds me of other things you've said about your life. Now, c'mon, start mixing paint."

As he squeezed ultramarine blue onto the palette, he asked, "So what is that supposed to mean: It reminds you of other parts of my life?"

I replied: "You've told me several stories from your relationship with Annie (his former girlfriend), work, and grad school, in which the whole point was how much you regret that you did not do things more carefully, and take your time and do it right."

Aaron seemed irritated. "Yeah, give me one example," he said defensively.

"Well, how about the managerial time study project that you told me about a couple of weeks ago," I said. "You told me yourself that you hurried. The result was a B, and you said that you knew you could have gotten an A if you had really applied yourself."

He dropped the paint stir in an exasperated motion and snapped: "So what! That was no big deal. My life doesn't revolve around a managerial time study on a fictitious corporation."

"No, Aaron, you are right," I said. "But the point is that if you handle the little things in a sloppy manner, it is likely that you'll treat more important things in the same way."

"Ah bull," he grunted.

I said, "Another example, and maybe a more important one, is how you described your intimacies with Annie."

"What in the world are you talking about?" he asked.

"Well, you told me that when you look back, you think that you were only interested in your own pleasure, not hers. You said, 'I just hurried through all the preliminaries,' and eventually that backfired."

In a hostile and sarcastic voice, he replied, "So you think that taking time to mix paint will bring Annie back?'"

I replied softly: "No, but it might help you pay more attention the next time around. I think you've gotten into the habit of rushing through life, Aaron, without focusing on anything. You are a sort of jack-of-all-trades. Is the dark blue ready? I think that your life deserves more care than you have given it. There is no substitute for quality work."

Aaron repainted the sky. When he completed covering the black with dark blue, he painted an orange-white harvest moon. He added touches of moonlight to the grass outside the house, and small highlights on the woman's face and robe. Aaron allowed himself to work on the painting for a few months. He made some mistakes and got frustrated, but was able to back up, think things through, and rework the images until he was satisfied. In a parallel sense, this describes what Aaron was doing intra-psychically: learning to struggle with attending to himself. He made some errors and got irritated, but was able to stop and gather himself, and remake his self-image. He learned to like what he saw in the canvas mirror.

I do not believe that such work could have been done in verbal psychotherapy. It was essential that Aaron encounter himself through the experience of making art. This is not to diminish the therapeutic benefit of the relationship that we developed over time. Certainly, our relationship had a curative impact, but it was intimately connected to the creative process and mastery of materials. It was in the context of the studio that our relationship existed.

It was equally significant that I insisted that he struggle with style and technique. Throughout our relationship, I encouraged him to use materials in a manner that honored them. Had I been willing to accept whatever artistic endeavor Aaron offered, I believe I would have exacerbated his negative self-view because he would have known that I was willing to settle for less than his best effort. There would have been no motivation on his part to struggle. That was the heart of his discomfort.

As art therapists, we have the unique capacity to simultaneously relate with the client, process, image, and product. This capacity allows us to move between the positions of consoler, teacher, beholder, and critic.

For many clients, the longing for meaning is a critical. As an art therapist, I believe that the role of art is a profound factor in establishing a sense of purposefulness. When the artist has genuinely struggled with the creative process and allowed the flow of imagery to proceed from within, he has said, in his most honest and clear voice, "This is who and what I am."

For too long in the art therapy profession, there has been a tendency to avoid looking too closely at the unique and authentic gifts of our client's and our own artworks from an aesthetic perspective. For art therapy to thrive, this oversight must be corrected. It is the aesthetics of the profession that depend most intimately on image and product, the lasting and tangible artifacts of the work. Art processes, images, and products distinguish the practice of art therapy from the routines of psychiatry, psychology, counseling, and social work.

Chapter 5

METAVERBAL THERAPY

Throughout the history of the art therapy profession, practitioners and theoreticians have been comfortable describing the discipline of art therapy as a non-verbal treatment modality. I, however, am not satisfied with this description of our work. I am concerned that defining art therapy as non-verbal portrays our work negatively. I believe that defining a profession in terms of what it is not, in this case not verbal, has an inadvertent detrimental effect on professional identity. I believe that we arts therapists should define ourselves positively by articulating what we are, rather than what we are not. I propose that we define art therapy as a metaverbal discipline. *Meta* is a prefix that means *beyond*. Thus, if we describe art therapy as a form of treatment that is metaverbal, we define our work as being *beyond words*.

The essence of our work as art therapists is found in our interactions with clients/artists, media, and process. In no way does what we say about this interaction change the nature of the art therapy process. The heart of the profession is experienced in moments that defy verbal description. Our words serve only to verify for the therapist the messages of the interaction and validate for the client that their messages have been heard. An art therapist's words do nothing to change the meanings of the interaction among client, media, and process. In a fundamental and radical sense, I believe that the most important work art therapists do is accomplished without speaking at all. Every time I find myself talking too much in an art therapy session, I worry that I have lost my center both as an artist and art therapist.

I have practiced art therapy for over 32 years in psychiatric hospitals, residential treatment programs, private practice, and educational settings. Having treated thousands of clients, I recall no occasion when the referring therapist or client sought my services because of my reputation as a conversationalist. Instead, clients have been referred to me or have sought me out because of the need for a metaverbal treatment approach. The extraordinary gift that art therapy has to offer clients is that the arts provide a therapeutic milieu that does not depend on words. In art therapy, doing forges therapy relationships, and making art is what we do. The world of health care is populated by disciplines in which words are the primary communicative device. Psychiatry, social work, psychology, and counseling all depend upon verbal exchanges with clients. Art therapists provide a therapy of imagination that does not rely solely on talking and is, therefore, refreshingly distinct from the approaches of our verbally-oriented colleagues.

It is in this spirit that I challenge art therapists to be skeptical of their longing to talk meaningfully with clients. I am not implying that I am silent in the creative arts therapy studio. I often talk with clients about the weather, last night's basketball game, or their favorite musician. I might in passing discuss an art exhibit I attended over the weekend. I may struggle out loud with my in-progress artwork, and I often share my reactions to my clients' artworks. Still, I do not see these interchanges as anything more than they are: good-natured small talk. The real therapeutic work, the soul work in art therapy, happens before any sounds in the shapes of words pass my lips.

The arts provide glimpses of the inner lives of my clients and myself. Every paint streak, each chalk line, and every slab of color, harmonious and dissonant, declare to the artist, beholders of the work, and humankind, "I am here and I have something to express."

The most the audience can do is catch a fleeting glimpse of the multi-layered communication of the creator. From such glimpses come the first stammering attempts at dialogue between beholder and artist. As we art therapists look at the works of our clients/artists, we must wrestle to uncover and focus the feelings, thoughts, and physical effort found in the soul of the piece. It is helpful to attempt to engage artworks as if they were sacred icons, conveyors of holy stories. As mysterious as this may sound, every time a client pulls color across a canvas, a proclamation is offered to the world: I am here, and I have something to show you. Too often in client's lives, the responses they have received from such declarations have been indifferent or malevolent. Thus, one task of art therapists is to see what clients are trying to say and respond in ways that honor those communications. It is not

easy to be in the company of expressions that go beyond words
(Figure 8).

If art therapy is truly metaverbal, one may wonder what role talking has in art therapy relationships. Vexing questions for students

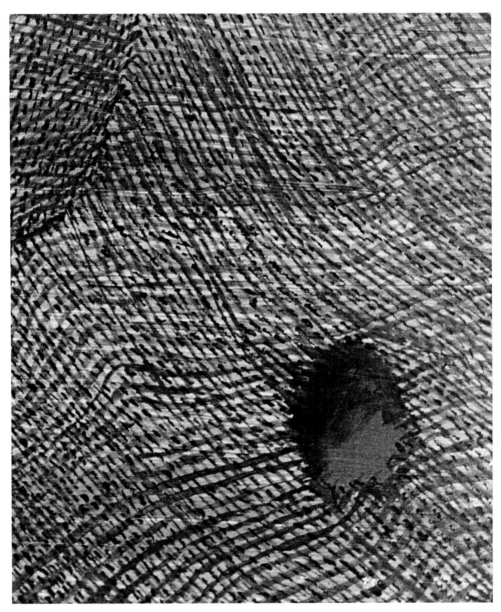

Figure 8. *Beyond Words*–Acrylic on masonite.

entering the arts therapy profession include: What is the role of talking? How much should I say? When should I say it? What should I say? Do I need to say anything at all? What if I can't think of anything to say?

As art therapists, we exist in the communities of helping professions, allied health professions, and educational professions. The therapies provided by psychiatrists, psychologists, counselors, and social workers depend upon spoken and written word. Yet art therapists by nature often find themselves dealing with feelings and ideas that cannot be sensibly or easily put into words. We operate in a world of images, colors, shadows, sensations, and intuitions.

In its early days, psychotherapy was termed *the talking cure*. One may ask if art therapy has a place in the realm of the psychiatrist, psychologist, and social worker, all of who use verbalization as their primary mode of interaction.

Words and Pictures from the Border

Dr. Lebeiko, a child psychiatrist, and I worked as co-therapists in an art psychotherapy group for more than a decade. The uniqueness of our joint venture lay in our ability to honor one another's disciplinary gifts: Dr. Lebeiko brought her tradition of verbal psychotherapy, while I contributed my respect for the unspoken power of artworks.

The clients selected for involvement in the group were often defensive, manipulative, and provocative adolescent girls with borderline personality disorder. Beyond the age, sex, and diagnostic criteria for entry into the group, we also sought clients who seemed to be slipping through the cracks in the hospital's therapeutic foundation. They were gliding through treatment as though coated in Teflon. No behavioral interventions or therapeutic interpretations went beyond their unhealthy psychological armor, and their verbal psychotherapists were frustrated.

One such client, Rachel, entered the group after having been in the hospital for nearly a month. She was a pretty, intelligent, outwardly cheerful 16-year-old. Prior to joining the group, she had remained distant and unattached to the treatment staff. She'd been hospitalized several times before coming to the facility, but had made minimal therapeutic progress. Her primary difficulties were identified as alcohol and drug abuse, intense enmeshment with her mother, sexual promiscuity, and teen-aged motherhood. She also had exhibited antisocial behaviors including vandalism, theft, and assaultive behavior, and criminal charges were pending for her in two states. It was of diagnostic interest that Rachel's mother had adopted Rachel's baby, further complicating their intense conflicted relationship.

Rachel's primary modes of relating to the treatment staff and her peers were twofold: She alternated between a coy, child-like superficiality, and a pseudo-mature and seductive style. Both ways of interacting served her well in keeping others at a safe distance from any genuine relationship.

On her first day in the art therapy group, the chasm between her outward demeanor and inner sense of self became apparent. As we went through the beginning ritual of sitting in a circle and checking in with each group member, Rachel commented, "I'm just great," and she flashed a pearly smile around the circle. When everyone had a turn, I announced that the directive for this session was, "Draw how you really feel." Rachel quickly gathered red and black chalk, and drew a slashing, spinning symbol on her 3″ x 3″ piece of brown paper. Later, as group members returned to the circle to share their artworks, I joked with Rachel about her drawing. I said, "Wow, that sure looks great!"

She smiled.

Dr. Lebeiko asked Rachel to give her drawing a voice. "What would it say, Rachel?"

Rachel's smile disappeared momentarily, and she remained silent. A few moments passed.

I asked the group, "As you listen to this image, what do you hear?"

One girl said, "I hear, I'm angry."

Another said, "Hurt."

Another said, "I'm lonely."

Rachel blurted out, "Ok, ok, so I feel like shit, so what?"

Dr. Lebeiko quickly moved to reassure Rachel by saying it was important to have a place to express how we really feel. Rachel's eyes brimmed, but she was not about to let anyone see her cry. The smile returned.

Some of Rachel's most significant work in the group took place while I was away from the hospital for a brief period. This was a difficult time for group members because it re-enacted abandonment themes that lay at the root of their dysfunction. The girls seized this opportunity and, in a pathological manner, acted out their hostility toward maternal figures on Dr. Lebeiko. To endure the attacks of each of these girls was no picnic for Dr. Lebeiko; however, it was a crucial opportunity to see their illnesses acted out on the therapeutic stage. It was grist for the mill. Rachel was the most vicious of the six. As she projected years of rage and frustration, her peers covertly elected her leader of the resistance movement.

Upon my return, as I saw each member in passing, there was a gush of, "Oh, God, group was so boring . . . so stupid . . . a waste of time." It was clear that the dynamic of devaluation of the mother, coupled with idealization of the father, was in full swing.

Our warm-up drawing in the next session was, "Catch me up on how life has been in this group." There was a flurry of ventilation on the walls of the expression room. Dr. Lebeiko and I made no comments as group members graphically spewed their hostility toward Dr. Lebeiko. Nor did we remark on their subtler message, "Please make it all better now." After everyone had a chance to vent about what they'd drawn, we moved on to the main theme of the day. The task was, "Draw a portrait of yourself and someone important to you."

I suspected that Rachel would draw either her mother or baby. What she drew, however, was a profound expression of the defensive psychological splitting process that actively engaged her. The drawing portrayed Rachel looking into a mirror, which reflected an ugly, fat, hateful, and lonely image.

As the two images of Rachel, one perfect and one horrible, began to dialogue, Rachel became tearful and vulnerable in the group for the first time. Her peers were at last able to see beyond the polished veneer that she had skillfully maintained. The mirror became a dominant visual metaphor for Rachel in sessions that followed, reflecting a more genuine image of her complete with good and bad qualities, both beautiful and blemished. The words used during her tenure in the group were few. The bulk of her work took place between herself, the paper, the chalk, and her images.

Amanda's Rage

When we announced to the group that Amanda would be joining us, there was a pronounced silence. Finally, one of the girls shared that she was frightened of Amanda. Amanda had a reputation on the adolescent unit. She was a large, masculine-appearing girl whose arms bore gruesome testimony to serious suicidal and self-mutilating efforts. She looked threatening. Her favorite pastime was lifting weights. She didn't like to talk, but she did draw. Having heard about her, my anticipatory fantasy about her involvement in the group was not pleasant. I envisioned resistance, testing of limits, intimidation, and conflict with other group members. (I have so little faith in the power of art sometimes.)

My fantasy fell apart with Amanda's first week in the group. Where I expected resistance, I found attachment. Where I anticipated limit-testing, I found compliance and investment in the process. Where I feared intimidation and conflict, I found a catalyst for meaningful engagement in the group. Clearly, Amanda's tough style and appearance were only that: style and appearance.

An illustration of this came on a day that the assigned task was, "Portray three significant events in your life." Remarkably, everyone's graphics included one reference to death and one symbolic portrait of loss. Amanda's drawing was extremely powerful in its simplicity. There were two tombstones beside a campfire. As Amanda began to share her images with the group, there was a marvelous metamorphosis. The silence in the room and attention paid to her by her peers were electric.

The first tombstone represented the death of a neighbor. She explained, "He was really like my father–like a father ought to be." The second symbolized her grandmother. She told us: "She was really my mom. My real mom was never around." The fire, Amanda said, represented the warmth and security she felt when she was with these two important people. "They made me feel like I was somebody," she said. "I had a place in their lives."

As another client talked about what it was like for her when her parents got divorced, Amanda chimed in: "Yeah, when my parents would fight, I'd just watch from the corner. I knew I didn't belong there."

In this session, Amanda metaphorically illustrated the crux of her difficulties. Her experience of anger as the force that kept her from belonging was the dynamic that pushed her to attempt to rigidly control her own rage. Her unfathomable fear of anger stemmed from a belief that to be angry would lead to having no sense of acceptance. She used all of her emotional energy to gain control and keep herself from exploding. The pressure mounted, she controlled, and the pressure continued to build. In subsequent sessions, she portrayed herself as a fire-breathing dragon. The equation was clear to Amanda: *anger = loss.* She had so much to be angry about, and her only avenue for release was in self-destructive and self-defeating behaviors such as cutting herself. The emotional payoff was that these actions eventually got her the attention she needed. The pattern had become: "If I tell anyone I'm angry, I will be rejected. But if I hurt myself, I will get attention and nurturance, plus everyone will know that I was angry." It was a great system that served her well.

The therapeutic task was to provide Amanda with alternative behaviors, nurturance, and acceptance like she had experienced with her grandmother and neighbor. Essentially, we wanted to help her learn to explode with color and line on the expressive room walls rather than implode on her arms. While words were a part of the process, they were not a major component of the therapeutic work with Amanda.

Tarri's Castle

Of all initial clients in my art therapy group with Dr. Lebeiko, Tarri was the most disturbed and disturbing. She was a moody, intelligent, volatile, bi-racial girl who was capable of being the center-of-attention comedienne who made everyone on the unit laugh. She could also withdraw from the world, acknowledging no one at all. I had seen her pound her fists wildly against her own face in a fit of rage.

Tarri had been adopted at age two. She was a cute girl with dark brown eyes. Her adoptive parents were blonde, blue-eyed people, with two older children of their own.

Tarri was a difficult client for the treatment team to understand. Her mood shifts were so dramatic that some thought she had multiple personality disorder. She complained of hearing voices, and some thought she was psychotic. Tarri had no way of describing or sharing her experience of the world. There were no words for her to offer. She was removed, distant, and suspicious of the staff. Nothing the treatment team did seemed to dent her psychological armor.

In the art therapy group, she seldom spoke. She responded to questions with yes-or-no answers. Graphically however, she poured on to the page images of the chaos she felt internally. Her startling pictures were always bound by thick, hard-edged lines. In one session, I asked the group to portray themselves in some other time and place, either past or future. Tarri drew a complicated scene from medieval days. She cast herself as a fair, helpless maiden who'd been trapped by a dragon. She also depicted a knight, but his armor was rusted, and he appeared powerless before the dragon.

In some ways, this drawing symbolized a dilemma of Tarri and each of her peers in the group. The image of the maiden seemed to represent a quality of innocent helplessness, or the child within each of them who had ceased to develop. The dragon encapsulated the rage that held the maiden prisoner. The rusty knight seemed to symbolize the futility of hope and a lack of faith in relationships.

In a later session, Tarri drew her "life as a landscape." She portrayed a nearly barren desert scene. There was a tiny pool near the center of the page, surrounded by a fence and high wall made of stone. As the group talked about the drawings that day, Tarri spoke haltingly of the emptiness and loneliness of her desert. When I asked her about the pool, she said, "It's really just a wish."

I responded, "Tarri, I believe that everything we draw is a partial self-portrait."

She blandly replied, "Oh."

I asked her to pretend that she was swimming in the pool.

Her eyes lit up as she described diving into cool, clear water. She told us that it was a secret place where only she could go. "This is my place," she said.

Dr. Lebeiko then led the group in a discussion of how much each member longed for a place that was her own where she could feel safe, secure, and as though she belonged.

This drawing marked a turning point for Tarri. The pool became a recurrent symbol. In the sessions that followed, she talked more openly about her longing for a home. The more she talked, the more it inspired others to share their feelings of abandonment and yearning.

Several weeks later, Tarri entered the room in a dismal mood. I tried to ask her what was going on but received no response. I asked her to draw what was on her mind. She divided her page in half. On one side, she drew a desolate landscape with a small house standing beside a road that led to a distant nothingness. The other side was filled with a lush garden/jungle scene. She sat staring at her picture for a few minutes, and then quietly said: "I've made up my mind, I can't go back to that house. I don't belong there. I never have." No other words were said. She sat, and she cried.

I cannot overemphasize the significance of this drawing. Tarri described the desolate landscape as her adoptive parents' plans and expectations for her. The garden represented her own goals. At a deeper level, these images presented a portrait of a square peg that had run out of energy trying to fit into a round hole. At times, there were words to frame her experience, but often the images simply spoke for themselves.

In our early days of co-therapy, Dr. Lebeiko would occasionally suggest that we spend more time talking in the group in the traditional open-ended, non-directive style in which she had been trained. Sometimes clients would complain that the art-making in the group was too predictable and boring. Despite my uneasiness with such verbally focused and non-directive approaches, for a time we did abandon the structure of doing art as the focus of the group.

We opened one session by announcing to the group that we had decided to shift gears and talk about whatever group members wished to discuss. The silence in the room was deafening. About 45 minutes of anxious and silent nothingness followed. The next session, the clients opened by complaining that the group was no longer helping them and that it was boring. Three of them stated that they were going to request to be removed from the group.

After several fruitless sessions, I again raised the issue of art structures in the post-group meeting with Dr. Lebeiko. In looking back on this phase of the group's life, there are at least two possible explanations of why so little happened. First, we had given in to the powerful resistance patterns of the clients. When they complained about the artistic processes as tiresome, they were really saying it was painful, hard work they wished to avoid. Their drawings inevitably brought them face-to-face with the struggles of their lives. Second, we had abandoned the non-directive approach too early; for example, perhaps our own anxiety pushed us to become more controlling so that something of value would occur in the sessions.

Both of these possible explanations may have some truth. Clearly, not much observable therapeutic work occurred in the group when we tried to rely on verbal, non-directive process. My bias is that it was the drawing process that provided a safe and secure environment in which to struggle metaphorically with the intense feelings of each group member. When the clients made art, powerful feelings leaked out onto the page, and once there, they could no longer be dodged or circumvented by defensive verbalization.

Regardless of which explanation is most valid, we did return to the use of artistic tasks in the structure of the group. Immediately, the group was able to refocus on feelings related to abandonment, self-hatred, and rage that each member struggled to endure.

Dr. Lebeiko and I have worked together for over 10 years. We eventually expanded our groups to include clients of many diagnostic categories. We included males, and our clients' average length of treatment dwindled from one year (when we began the group) to slightly more than two weeks. Despite these radical shifts in group composition and duration of treatment, the work remained essentially the same. The role of words in the art therapy group process may best be described as one of honoring and validating the artistic expressions of clients, nothing less, nothing more. Art therapy truly is metaverbal.

Chapter 6

THE NATURE OF THE WORK

One surprising aspect of the field of art therapy to the novice student is the inherent presence of conflict in both clinical and academic environments. Perhaps the surprise element is related to motivations that bring students into the field, including love and a longing to serve humankind. The intense oppositional forces that novices confront as they begin their lives as art therapists often take them aback. Conflict, in the way I am using it, refers to the opposition of persons or forces that give rise to dramatic action in drama or fiction.

Art therapy students often come to the discipline wearing rose-colored glasses, full of good will and best intentions. Art has soothed them, and they want to use it to help others. Soon, however, they must contend with the ill-tempered client who defeats their warmest maneuvers, and the professor who demands that they document their papers in APA format. They are confronted with the peer in graduate school who thrives on competition and stirs their worst fears of inadequacy.

Conflict is everywhere in the world of the art therapist. The client seeks therapy, not in a spirit of harmony and peace, but out of dissonance and emotional turmoil. There are always interdisciplinary rivalries, philosophic disagreements, and institutional politics. Even within the art therapy profession, heated disputes have occurred throughout history.

To deal with conflict, I find it helpful to work toward an understanding of the role of discord in human existence. Life begins in struggle. Pre-birth hours are filled with hesitant, painful movement away from the safety and warmth of the womb, toward the bright, cold uncertainty of life outside. The birth process is the first conflict in a person's life. As such, it symbolizes much of what is to follow: a life composed of one conflict after another.

Reflect on some developmental tasks and existential concerns that await the newborn. There are the initial struggles to communicate one's need for food, dryness, warmth, fondling, and love, all without the advantage of speech. Then come encounters with the outside world, parents, siblings, and peers. There are inevitable feelings of loss and rejection the first time that a mother leaves her child in the care of another. There is the first day of kindergarten and the first run-in with the school bully. Then come the first bodily and psychological changes of puberty. The first date, the first rejection, and the first move away from home are all challenging conflicts. Then come marriage and the birth of one's own children, and on and on the conflict cycle spins. The beginning to the end of our lives are flooded with inevitable changes and unavoidable conflict.

A finer attribute of humankind is our resilience in the face of surrounding instability. Our capacity to adapt, change, and struggle with conflict, both internal and external, is remarkable. It is a tenet of existentialism that the worth of people's existence is determined by how they respond to conflict and anguish.

The individual's ability to creatively contend with the skirmishes of life marks the difference between a productive, authentic existence, and a life marked with defeat and emptiness. This capacity may be described as a coping skill, defense mechanism, adaptability, or optimism. For our purposes, I will call it the capacity for creative conflict resolution.

Let me turn to my theological tradition to describe the foundation of creative conflict resolution. In the biblical Book of Genesis (Revised Standard Version) we are confronted with an image of God as Creator: "In the beginning God created . . ." (1:1). Within a few passages, we read that God created humans in His own image (1:26). At this point in the Bible, the only thing we know of God is that He creates. One may presume, then, that this is one primary characteristic that human beings share with God: We create.

In modern times, the notion of people as creative beings has diminished. It is as if creativity is seen as a private attribute of the artist, entertainer, or scientist. We seldom speak of the creative potential of the average person who works on an assembly line. Those who define themselves as creative often indulge in a form of elitism, excluding the common person from the ranks of creativity. The severity of such an error is not only that the "creative people" delude themselves, but also that frequently the world at large accepts the prejudice.

It hasn't always been this way. Prior to the industrial revolution, every man and woman had to use creativity to survive. When faced with the realities of making shelter, food, clothing, tools, and entertainment, people created or perished. The conflicts were ever present, and the capacity for creative resolution determined one's fate.

In this age of mass manufactured housing, processed food, designer clothing, and the instant diversion of television, our conflicts are less material and apparent, but no less threatening. They are even more malevolent because of their subtlety.

Art history teaches that lasting works of great art are those that wrestle with confounding themes of existence. Humanity's relation to God, nature, war, sexuality, society, and self are repeated motifs. From the prehistoric cave paintings of France and Michelangelo's Sistine Chapel to Picasso's *Guernica* and Dali's *Last Supper,* the scenes are those of humankind's struggle to resolve conflict.

A mark of emotional and mental health is the ability to contend with the struggle and anguish of life. People who come to art therapists, whether in a private practice or psychiatric hospital and regardless of diagnosis or personality type, are in conflict. They have been unable to successfully cope, fully defend, or satisfactorily adapt. Their lives bear the scars of having been figuratively (and sometimes literally) beaten and battered by their struggle with life.

The task of art therapists is to call upon the inherent creative potential of clients. We must enlist creativity as an ally in the complicated work of unraveling the snarled yarn of the client's life, freeing the person from the snare of victimization.

In my first year of graduate school, I suffered from a malady common among my peers. I suspected that I was somehow less intelligent and less sophisticated than everyone else in school. For months, I wrestled with whether to drop out of school. I finally decided to share my concerns with my academic advisor. After I told him I thought I was "in over my head," he began to laugh. I flushed with anger and resentment. Then he told me that I was the third student that week who was feeling overwhelmed.

"Bruce," he said. "You are suffering because you haven't figured out the higher education game yet. You see, it's not a matter of teaching students facts or dates, or even the ideas of famous people. The point of being here is to learn how to learn." A light came on in my head. I'd been focusing my attention on specifics of course material while ignoring the whole process of learning to think creatively about any given problem or situation.

As art therapists, we are in an intriguing position with clients. One of our primary tasks is making art in the company of clients. By doing this, we call out clients' creative potential. As artists, we know that conflict is inherent in painting, sculpting, molding, dancing, and making. By virtue of all that has been created in the name of art, we stand at a pivotal point in the acceptance and expression of conflict. Doing art is a natural method of evoking and sharing feelings and ideas that essentially oppose each other. As art therapists, we foster in our clients a belief that they are capable of creative resolution for problems in art production. At the same time, the capability to struggle with other areas of conflict in clients' lives is serendipitously nourished.

Art therapists do not necessarily need to focus attention on one specific conflict, but rather on the nature of conflict as a symbol of life in process. If this attitude can be engendered in the client, particular struggles will no longer be avoided but, rather, embraced as a validation of life itself.

AN ILLUSTRATION

I'd been on vacation for three weeks. It was my first day back at the psychiatric hospital, and as I walked into the art therapy studio, I quickly became aware of Jenny's hostile glare. She'd been admitted to the hospital while I was away, and although I had not met her, I knew from the staff meeting earlier that morning that she was 16 years old, and had been angry and resistive in the studio. Out of the corner of my eye, I saw her squirt a stream of white glue onto a piece of Masonite board. She proceeded to randomly place mosaic tiles on the board, paying no attention to color or design.

I approached her and introduced myself. "Hello, my name is Bruce," I said. "I've been on vacation for awhile. Who are you?"

She turned toward me and, with one fist clenched, asked, "What do you care?" This response triggered snickers from her peers.

One of the other adolescent clients said, "This is Jenny, she came in last week."

Figure 9. *The Studio at Harding Hospital*–Photograph by Bruce Moon.

"Thanks," I said. "Now, Jenny, what are you working on here?"

She shoved the board across the table in my direction without speaking.

"Ah, a mosaic," I said.

Jenny turned to her friend and smirked, "What is he talking about?"

I replied: "I'm talking about your work, Jenny, and I am curious about your theme. What are you trying to express? We want artists to work on important things in this studio. You know, things like feelings or events that have been significant in your life."

She snarled, "You want me to draw a pig?"

I learned later that she had been referred to the hospital from the juvenile court system. She had several criminal charges pending, and the judge wanted her to undergo psychiatric evaluation.

"No," I said. "But I . . ."

Jenny glared at me and said, "I don't give a shit what you want."

"Jenny, you are going to have to not talk that way in the studio," I said. "We need this to be a safe and comfortable place for everybody. Swearing makes it hard on everyone."

"Are you fuckin' for real?" she asked.

I replied: "I'm serious about this, Jenny. Now, can we talk about your artwork?"

She grimaced and said: "It's nothing. I'm just doing it."

My mentor, Jones, would often say that clients always express what they need to express. The difficult part for art therapists is to grasp the meaning of the expression. In this brief encounter, I sensed that Jenny had laid out several important themes of her life. First, there was the random and chaotic quality to the art piece she was creating. Second, she had dramatically enacted her disregard and disrespect for adult authority figures. Third, she had indirectly indicated that important aspects of her life were in the hands of others like the police.

I thought about these three thematic elements and said: "Well, we'll have to start something that has meaning for you. I'll stop back in a few minutes." I turned and headed back to an easel where I had a canvas in progress.

As I started to work on my painting, I overheard Jenny sneer to her friend, "I can't do a damn thing with him bitching at me."

"That's it, Jenny," I said. "I am going to have to send you back to the unit. We really can't have talk like that here in the studio. We'll try again tomorrow."

The next day went much like the first session. She was again sent back to the unit in response to her negative, devaluing, and hostile behavior. As she was being escorted from the building, I said, "Tomorrow, let's build a canvas together and get going on a painting." She did not reply.

To my surprise, Jenny entered the studio the following day and announced that she was ready to work. We began with my showing her how to use the miter saw to cut 2 x 2s for her stretcher frame. She whined that the wood was too hard, and the saw was too dull. I replied, "Jenny, let's struggle with it."

After the frame was constructed, I taught her how to stretch canvas. She asked: "Could you leave me alone? I can do this."

"All right," I said, "but let me know when you get to the corners; they can be tricky."

When she called me back to the room where she'd been working, I saw a too-loose, too-wrinkled canvas. "Jenny, this isn't tight enough," I said. "Let's take it off and start over."

"What?" she groaned. "It's Tom's fault. He came in here talking to me and . . ."

"Jenny, there is no substitute for paying attention to your work and taking your time," I said.

"Why isn't this good enough?" she asked.

I began pulling staples and said: "Because you are worth more than this. C'mon, give me a hand."

"I can't do this," she exclaimed.

"I have faith in you," I replied.

"I can't do this," she protested.

"Trust me," I said.

During the weeks that Jenny was in the hospital, our relationship shifted from focusing on conflict with authority and boundary setting, to one marked by mutual interest and support. I worked alongside as she cut wood, constructed a frame, stretched and primed canvas, learned painting techniques, painted over, critiqued, re-worked, and finally signed her canvas. She created an image of a desert plain leading to a desolate mountain range against an empty magenta sky. It was an intense lonely painting, and a heartrending metaphoric self-portrait. This was not easy work. Withstanding the initial hostility and resistance of clients like Jenny who you wish to help is not pleasant, and yet it is frequently an important aspect of therapeutic work.

What is the nature of the work that art therapists do? It is often painful, emotionally bruising blistering, stretching, and demanding. No one seeks therapy because of good feelings. On the contrary, therapy is typically sought as a last resort when other avenues for alleviation of discomfort have been tried. Therefore, the work of therapy is seldom reflective of happiness, fulfillment, or peace of mind. Art therapy does, however, typically proceed through three phases: resistance, working through, and termination. These phases are not linear and discreet, but rather fluid and intermingling. For the sake of description, however, I will discuss them in sequence.

The Resistance Phase of Art Therapy

Usually the guideposts of therapeutic work are rage, loss, hurt, denial, abandonment, anxiety, guilt, and emptiness. The roads these guideposts demarcate are hard to travel, and clients typically are forced to walk them by life circumstances beyond their control. Clients are understandably wary, guarded, hesitant to trust, and quick to lash out defensively. On such roads of anguish, the first steps of the therapeutic journey are taken. The art therapist must not be put off by the resistance maneuvers of clients because this is how clients begin to share their stories. Such work is not pleasant, easy, or comfortable for art therapists. There have been many Jennys in my professional life: children filled with loathing for adults and themselves. With rage, loneliness, and damaged souls, they have been forced to fend for themselves in a world all too willing to abuse their vulnerabilities.

In the treatment of emotional disturbed adolescents and adults, one early task for art therapists is to establish clear consistent boundaries to create a safe and predictable milieu. It was natural and logical for Jenny to resist and distrust me. Many of her life experiences with adult authority figures had led her to believe that I would in some way be harmful to her. In response, it consciously maintained a neutral affective manner and established the boundaries of our relationship by setting clear limits on her self-defeating and negative behaviors. It was not pleasant to confront Jenny's resistive behaviors, but it was necessary.

In the early stages of art therapy, one should contain and respond to clients' resistance maneuvers. No client–child, adolescent, adult, or geriatric–seeks art therapy when feeling good. The act of entering therapy is an acknowledgement that the client's life is painful and distressing. Even when clients commence therapy voluntarily and are outwardly motivated and anxious to begin, it is still human nature to resist entering into the pain that therapy often involves.

In my life, I have broken my Achilles heel, jaw, and the fifth metatarsal in both feet. Each time I broke a bone, there was an immediate pain signaling that something was wrong and needed attention. After awhile, the pain would diminish, and as I would lie on the table awaiting the results of the x-rays, I could almost convince myself that no bone was broken. Then the doctor would enter the room and deliver the bad news. Every time, the physician ended up realigning a bone so that it could heal properly. Setting the bone always reignited the pain of the break.

Commencing therapy can be like setting a broken bone, and despite the good intentions of art therapists, clients cannot help but associate them with the pain of life. Nearly all clients resist art therapy; why wouldn't they? It is the nature of the work of art therapists that we must deal with the resistance of the client.

The Working Through Phase of Art Therapy

The second phase of art therapy, the working through phase, is marked by a significant decrease in overt and covert resistance maneuvers. Similar to the resistance phase, the working through phase is often not put into words, but rather is observed in the behaviors of clients. The working through phase is a time of intense work as clients begin to exchange negative self-concepts for more positive views of self that come from artistic expression of feelings and the relationship with the art therapist. How clients perceive art therapists' positive regard for them, genuine interest, and ability to understand and honor pain, is a catalyst for helping clients rework internal views of self. As art therapists encounter the battered and bruised inner worlds of clients and respond in ways that are different than others in the past have done, self-regard is altered. Essential to the curative process is the client's experience of being understood by the art therapist. Inherent in this understanding is the client's belief that despite the painful, angry, and horrible feelings harbored within, the art therapist accepts and cares for the client as is. The art therapist's ability to understand is fostered by the capacity to be with and attend to the images and meanings of clients' artworks.

Jerry, the Wild Boy

Jerry was a wild kid: a terror, everyone said. He was 11 years old when I first met him. I'd read his medical chart, and I knew about his past. His mother had left him in the bathroom of a bar when he was a year-and-a-half old. He'd been shuffled around the foster care system, spending time in several different homes before he was adopted. Although his adoptive parents had the best intentions for Jerry, his "monstrous behavior" had so frightened and alienated them that they were considering returning custody of Jerry to the county department of children's service. Adopted at the age of five-and-a-half, he'd always been difficult to live with, but he'd made his parents' lives especially miserable for the 18 months prior to his admission to the psychiatric hospital. He'd been aggressive toward his peers at school and suspended several times. He'd set fire to the curtains in his house, causing thousands of dollars of damage. He'd run away. Sometimes, Jerry wouldn't talk for days at a time, and other times, he would not be quiet. Jerry was a wild kid: a terror.

Jerry had been in the hospital about three weeks when I received a referral from his primary therapist asking that I evaluate him to see if he might benefit from individual art therapy. I met with Jerry for an art therapy assessment session, and was immediately fascinated by his artworks and rage. In the evaluation session, I offered him a range of artistic materials and told him that he could create whatever he wanted. He gave me a sidelong glance, as if to ask if I was serious. I assured him that he could use whatever materials were in the room, and that he could draw or paint whatever he wanted.

Jerry quickly gathered all of the tempera paints and arranged them on the table before him. He asked, "Can I paint on that black paper?" He pointed toward a roll of 36" wide black construction paper leaning against one wall in the corner of the studio. Again, I assured him that he could use whatever materials he preferred. He pulled several feet of black paper from the roll and began to paint. Jackson Pollack and the *Peanuts* character Pig Pen both would have been proud of Jerry's efforts that morning. When he was finished, the studio was a disaster. Paint was everywhere.

Jerry titled his work, *The Blob Man.* He said, "This is what I see when I close my eyes at night." The painting he'd created was chaotic, confusing, and overwhelming to look at. Upon the black background, he had swirled rivers of red, purple, brown, and blue. Over these he had poured streams of yellow and orange. Finally, as a crowning touch, he carefully dripped countless beads of white and gray. He had worked so intently that there was little time left in the session.

As I went about the chores of cleaning brushes and paint cups, I sighed, "It must be hard to sleep with all that going on."

"Yeah," he said. "Sometimes I hardly sleep at all in the night. But don't tell my mom, she'd be mad if she knew." Then he spit onto his painting and rubbed his saliva into the paint with his hand. He looked up at me and asked, "Can I leave now?"

I turned toward him, "Yes, Jerry, you can go if that's what you want to do, but I wouldn't mind it if you wanted to help me clean up." To my surprise he picked up a wet sponge and began to work on the paint splatters he'd made on the worktable.

Nothing more was said during that session, but by the time we'd gotten the studio back into proper condition, I felt sure that I could work with Jerry, and that he would benefit from the art therapy process. In the months that followed, he frequently tested my patience and determination. It seemed that many events from Jerry's past had taught him to be suspicious of adults. He had no desire to be hurt again, so he enacted a host of resistance behaviors.

The treatment team responsible for planning, implementing, and monitoring Jerry's hospital and outpatient treatment postulated that his behavioral and emotional difficulties stemmed from early experiences of psychological deprivation, physical neglect, and trauma of abandonment. Our working hypothesis was that his emotional development had been stalled somewhere around the level of a two-year-old. That phase of development is characterized by the child's emerging sense of independence. In this phase, there is a need to separate from the primary nurturer, in this case Jerry's mother, and also a need to frequently return to the nurturer for emotional support and security. The treatment team sensed that Jerry had never been able to move past this early stage because of instability in his relationships with caregivers. We theorized that this developmental arrest accounted for his aggressive behaviors directed most often at parental figures and situations like school that symbolized movement away from the primary caregiver.

From this understanding, we formulated a treatment plan that provided Jerry with multiple reparative experiences intended to help him work through his early trauma and stimulate developmental progress. We had no illusions that this would be an easy or quick cure. Jerry's problems were serious, and his self-defeating coping behaviors were a nearly life-long pattern. Compounding the problems was the fact that Jerry was only eleven years old. To expect him to be able to work in individual therapy based primarily on verbal exchanges was unrealistic. A regimen of action-oriented treatment modalities was designed for him.

Jerry was in the hospital for eight or nine weeks. The hospital provided him with a safe, predictable, and nurturing environment. As the weeks passed, the recreation therapist, music therapist, play therapist, and educational tutor each reported a gradual decrease in Jerry's resistance. As he became increasingly cooperative and trusting of the staff, his defensive distancing maneuvers faded. He was discharged from the hospital with a plan for ongoing art therapy and weekly sessions with the play therapist. He had begun the working through phase of his therapy.

Jerry was sitting at a table in the art therapy studio working on an acrylic painting. The scene he was trying to depict was a dark room featuring two doors on one wall, each opening to a long hallway. He had just completed a silhouette of a human figure huddled on the floor in the corner of the room. He slammed his brush on the table and exclaimed, "This looks like crap!"

I turned from my easel, lay down my palette, and went to his side. "Hmmm, I see what you mean, Jerry," I said. "I think it is the person. You only used black. Everything else in the picture has color. I think the black looks out of place."

"I don't mean just that," he said. "This whole thing looks like . . ."

"It would probably look better if you tried to make the pants the color of old blue jeans," I said. (Jerry always wore faded denims.) "And, maybe you could make the shirt be the color of your *Lakers* shirt." I picked up his painting and placed it on the easel I'd been using. I stepped away a few feet, called him to my side, and said: "Yes, I think that will work, Jerry. You've really got an interesting piece going here. The hallways give it an eerie and lonely feeling." I returned the painting to where he'd been working at the table and said: "Let me know if you need any help with the purple for the shirt. I think I'd start with the indigo and add just a touch of white."

"But I can't do that," he lamented.

I went back to my painting, smiled at him, and said: "I have faith in you Jerry. I'll help you when you need it."

Without further protest, Jerry went to the paint cabinet and gathered his colors. Later in the session, he asked for help mixing the yellow-gold that he wanted for the trim on the *Lakers* shirt. I don't think he really needed my help mixing the color, but his request provided a way for him to get the emotional support that he needed in a way that he could accept.

Variations of this interaction between Jerry and me occurred repeatedly. These experiences were curative for him. In looking back, I think it was crucial that I offered him opportunities to work independently to metaphorically toddle off and explore the world. It was also critical that I was there for him when he returned to my side for emotional support.

To understand the significance of these interactions, imagine the toddler who leaves the room where his mother is. He goes to the playroom, occupies himself for several minutes, then realizes he is alone. He makes his way back to his mother for assurance that his world is secure. The mother stops what she is doing, bends down, smiles and coos, gives the child a hug, and he is off to explore the world again.

During the working through phase of art therapy, Jerry repeatedly experienced situations metaphoric of toddling situations. Each successful venture helped form the foundation of his capacity to resolve the developmental fixation. As he became more self-assured from the successes he had in the art therapy studio and our relationship, his aggressive behaviors toward his adoptive parents and peers diminished. Note that art therapy at this level cannot necessarily be put into meaningful verbal constructs. Jerry had to learn by doing. That was the nature of the work.

The working through phase of art therapy is often the most gratifying for art therapists. It is in the working through phase that changes in client's behaviors and self-image are seen. In this phase, clients are able to view their lives as stories they had a major part in writing. Clients take responsibility for difficulties and successes. These characteristics make the working through phase of treatment appealing to the therapist. Such work is not possible without the earlier struggle with resistances, and accomplishments of the working through phase are incomplete without the third phase of termination.

The Termination Phase of Art Therapy

Art therapists should understand that termination is a process not event. The termination phase of therapy is critical because during this period, clients demonstrate the strength and enduring nature of the changes they have made. Clients often experience a period of increased anxiety, and termination is sometimes perceived as another abandonment. When art therapy goes well, clients develop trust in the art therapist because they feel cared for and safe. It is understandable, then, that the approaching end of the relationship is accompanied by emotional turmoil.

As a result of termination apprehension, the early stages of this phase may be marked by temporary regressions as the client struggles to cope with anxiety and loss related to saying good-bye to the art therapist. This anxiety is exacerbated if the therapy has taken place in a hospital or residential treatment facility, for not only is the client leaving the art therapist, but the client is also saying farewell to doctors, nurses, activity therapists, social workers, and peers. On one hand, ambivalent feelings are prevalent because the client looks forward to getting out of the hospital and back to normal life. On the other hand, the client has formed significant relationships and had meaningful experiences, and I hope has come to feel better about life.

In my years of doing therapeutic work, I have observed many clients terminate. This process of termination can be characterized by four dominant patterns or metaphoric themes:

1. *I will get mad at you, you will be angry with me, and I will feel no pain when I leave you.* The meta-message underlying this style of termination is that clients believe it will be too painful to say good-bye and to really let the therapist know how they feel. This is fairly typical with adolescent clients for whom acknowledgment of their feelings toward adults, especially warm ones, is often difficult. When dealing with clients in the termination phase of treatment who manifest this style of coping, the art therapist should avoid being cast aside by the client's anger. Rather, the art therapist must respond in a way that honors the anger, as well as the pervasive fear of loss that engenders it.

2. *I will withdraw from you early, so that when I leave I will not miss you.* The meta-message here is a belief by clients that if they are out of sight, they will be out of mind. Their withdrawal is often misinterpreted as being a rejection of the therapy experience. In this instance, the art therapist must not become overly solicitous, but rather remain accepting and responsive to the client's imagery and behavior, yet affectively neutral.

3. *Wasn't this wonderful, I'm glad I met you, and you've really changed my life.* Clients coping with their anxiety in this way are idealizing the treatment experience as a way of defending themselves from the reality of how post-treatment life will be. A magical wish is often present that now that they have completed therapy, their lives will be forever smooth sailing. This, of course, is seldom the case. By complimenting the art therapist, clients keep the focus of the last several sessions off of the difficulties that lay ahead.

4. *I will use this time to honor the work that we have done together.* Clients who use this form of the termination process take the opportunity to summarize the work that has been done in the context of the therapy relationship. Realistic recounting of the meanings created between client and therapist marks this approach to the process of

saying good-bye. There is no effort by the client to glorify or deval-ue the importance of the relationship. This authentic engagement in the ending process is generally viewed as a positive prognostic indi-cator.

Several notable signposts mark productive therapeutic process. The art therapist should be vigilant in looking for these as the relationship unfolds. For therapy to be successful, clients must navigate through the resistance phase. The skilled art therapist knows that this is being done when clients can take ownership of difficulties without undue blaming of others for their misfortunes. One of my art therapy students described this as such: "It's as if the client had been watching his life on videotape. Suddenly, he realized that it was more like a play and that he was the playwright." The working through phase is discernible as the client becomes interested in self-disclosure, introspection, and meaningful behavioral change. Finally, therapy, like all things, must come to an end. The fruits of the work are harvested as the client is able to define significant qualities of relationships, including feelings, per-ceptions, and meanings. The harvest may or may not be a process put into words. In my experience in hospital settings, typically such things went unspoken. Instead, they were acted out symbolically through drawings, paintings, and sculptures. This is the nature of the work.

The Story of Jan

When I first met Jan, she had the striking good looks and poise of a professional model. I (B. L. Moon, 1990) wrote about her hospital art therapy in my first book:

> Jan had been raised in a well-to-do family. She said that everything she wanted had always been hers for the asking. To the outside observer she had everything that should have made her happy. Her family loved her, all her material needs were supplied, she had an exciting life . . . and yet Jan had tried to kill herself. That brought her to the hospital and into the art therapy studio. (p. 64)

A few weeks into her hospitalization, Jan began to paint. After sev-eral aborted attempts at portraits, still life, and landscapes, Jan was dejected and frustrated. She asked to have her daily schedule changed so that she could be in a ceramics group and withdraw from the painting studio. I was concerned that her desire to get out of the painting group was an expression of avoidance, although I was unsure of what she was avoiding. After some negotiation, Jan and I agreed that she would leave the studio after she completed a painting. Although she agreed to this, she was nonetheless irritated by the delay. She sarcastically asked, "What do I have to paint, boss?"

Without responding to her subtle hostility, I suggested she work on the theme of good-bye. I told her she could use any style she wanted, but it was important that she finish. What emerged was strikingly different from her other clumsy attempts at mimicking another artist's style or reproducing a photograph in acrylic paint. She began by painting the entire canvas dark red. She then covered the bottom half with black and, leaving a sliver of intense red, she painted the top portion deep indigo. The visual effect of this painting was powerful. The red pulsated behind the darker colors, evoking the image of a wound. Here at last was a real work, not something sugar-coated or blemish-free. It was a raw and painful expression of feeling. The piece screamed for comment, and her peers in the studio responded to the call. Some praised the painting, some patted Jan on the back, and others looked at it silently before moving on to their own work.

On the day she signed the painting, I asked, "Do you want to talk about this piece?"

She said, "No, I just want to stretch another canvas and get to work on another painting." I went in search of the staple gun.

I'd had no contact with her for two years after she'd left the hospital. Her psychiatrist telephoned one afternoon to inquire if I would see Jan in my private practice. I had fond memories of Jan, and I agreed to meet with her early the next week to explore the possibility of renewing our treatment relationship. Jan's doctor informed me that she had been married and divorced since last I'd seen her. The marriage had been impulsive and unhappy from the beginning. He told me he was frustrated because she was often flippant and superficial about her life. He said, "She tells me they made a beautiful couple, but they just didn't like each other very much." He also informed me that Jan had suggested contacting me. It was their hope that she might be able to engage more seriously in her therapy through involving, once again, in the art processes.

Jan came to my office the following Tuesday. After getting reacquainted, we began an artistic pilgrimage that lasted nearly two years.

During that time, Jan worked on painting after painting, each new one delving deeper than the last. It was as if the process of painting created a metaphoric onion for her. Each new creative act peeled away another level, showing increasingly precious aspects of her complex self. Raging inner fires succeeded images of beauty and ugliness. Deep sorrowful pools quenched the fires and, in turn, evaporated beneath a harsh inner sun that baked a barren desert. Layer after layer, image upon image, the prismatic person beneath her flawless shell emerged.

As her inward exploration unfolded, I had little to do. Jan did all the hard work. Hillman (1989) describes images as necessary angels waiting for a response. Jan was greeted by many angels in the years that she came to me for art therapy, and she responded to them.

She'd been attending sessions regularly for almost two years when she brought a painting of an old small town train depot. She had restricted her palette to gentle umbers and warm subtle yellows and oranges. The painting had a dusty forlorn quality. As she worked on this, she mused that it reminded her of the small town in western Ohio where her grandparents lived. She recalled taking a train ride to Lima, Ohio, with her grandpa. She sighed, "I always wanted to stand on the wooden walk in front of the depot and greet some long awaited visitor arriving on the train."

"Jan," I said, "I wonder what it would be like to get on the train and head off into the sunset?"

"You mean, be the one who was leaving the people at the station?" she replied.

"Yes," I said. "What would that be like?"

She grimaced and said: "I don't know. I never leave anyone. They always leave me."

Jan was fairly quiet for the rest of that session. She asked for technical help on one small section of the piece, but that seemed perfunctory, and I believe she did not really need my assistance. In the silences, I knew that something had passed between us during the interaction around the train station, but I was unclear just what it was.

I took my notes from the session to my next meeting with my supervisor. I described the uneasy silences, reconstructed our conversation as best I could, and tried to describe the painting Jan was working on. When I'd finished recounting the session, my supervisor asked me how I felt.

I said, "Warm but sort of lonely."

He replied, "Maybe she's trying to tell you that she's getting ready to terminate therapy." As soon as I heard this interpretation, I suspected it was correct.

I asked, "Do you think I should raise the subject with her at our next session?"

He suggested that I maintain the neutral stance I had adopted during the course of her therapy. "She'll put it into words or pictures when she is ready to," he said.

When Jan returned to the studio the following week, she brought only her sketchbook. I inquired as to the whereabouts of the painting, and she remarked in an offhand manner, "I forgot it." The painting continued to be "forgotten" for the next two sessions. It reappeared on a bright afternoon in late October. Jan had added small details to the painting: highlights and shadows. She also brought her sketchbook and showed me a roughly drawn figure of a man standing beside railroad tracks. Although the drawing seemed hesitant and lightly done, it appeared as if the man was waving toward the vanishing point between the two rails on the distant horizon. "Ah, I see you've been working," I said.

"Yes," she replied. "I've had this painting sitting in my dining room for the longest time. I hadn't touched it. Then the other night, I got the urge to add the man." She pointed to the sketchbook.

"He's waving?" I asked.

"Yes, he's been left behind," she sighed. The rest of the session was spent painting and discussing techniques, an art show that had recently opened at the Columbus Museum of Art, and how things were going for Jan at work. At the end of session, as I was filling out an appointment reminder card, Jan asked, "Could we not meet again until two weeks from now?"

"That would be fine," I said. "Are you busy next week?"

"No," she said. "I just thought I'd like to try coming a little less often for awhile." Two weeks later, Jan called to cancel our session. She scheduled an appointment for the following week. When she arrived for the session, the painting and her sketches were in the same condition as they'd been three weeks prior.

"I've felt stuck," she lamented. "I can't seem to get his arm right." She pointed toward the upraised waving arm of the man. "Could you stand up for a minute and pose like that while I sketch it again?" she asked.

I turned toward her and said, "I've wondered if maybe that figure was supposed to be me." Jan offered no reply. She focused her attention on her sketchbook.

A couple of minutes later, she said, "Okay, I'm done drawing; you can sit down."

"You missed our appointment last week," I said.

"I know, something came up," she replied.

Nothing more was said for several minutes. When I approached the easel where she was working, I could not help but notice that the figure of the man had clothing similar to mine.

Jan put her brushes in the water container, sat down, and said: "Yes, Bruce, I think this guy is you. I think he's waving good-bye to me."

I shifted my gaze to the painting and said, "I wonder how he feels waving good-bye?"

Jan replied, "Oh, I think he's sad and happy both."

"How is that possible?" I asked.

She paused and said: "He's sad because he won't get to see the woman on the train very often anymore. She's moving away. And he's happy for her too, because she is happy."

"I see," I said. "Where is she going?"

"She's moving out west to Colorado," she replied.

I quoted Paul Simon (1983), "Everybody loves the sound of a train in the distance, everybody thinks it's true."

Jan shifted her weight on the stool. "I think it's about time, Bruce," she said. "I think I'm ready to move on."

I replied: "Everything ends, Jan. Maybe your painting is a symbol of endings. Should we talk about you stopping therapy?"

She turned away and said, "I think I'll just paint."

Over the next few weeks, the painting continued to develop (Figure 10). Details were added. She painted an easel behind the window in the depot, a symbol of our time together. A faded circus poster was added to the weathered wall of the station, recalling a particularly difficult period of Jan's therapy in which she felt herself to be false, as well as a painted clown. For the most part, Jan and I spoke of artistic techniques, shadows and light, and washes and highlights. Still, the painting became a symbolic object, an icon of sorts representing our relationship. Images of pain, sadness, anger, loneliness, joy, and hope emerged. It was, in dramatic fashion, an imaginal record of our time together. Several times, Jan wondered aloud what I would do if she

Figure 10. *Ready to Move On*–Acrylic on canvas.

"just disappeared." I would remind her that saying good-bye was a process not event.

Our process ended when Jan signed the painting. It was, for me, both a haunting and warmly nostalgic artwork. As she spoke of it during our last session together, she recalled moments of tenderness and silliness that had passed between us.

I have wondered, from time to time, how Jan is doing in her new life. I hope that all is going well for her because she deserves good things in her life. Now and again, I feel as if I am a professional good-bye sayer. It is almost frightening to me to think of how many significant relationships I have established over the past three decades only to bid them farewell. It is the nature of the work. The whole point of establishing the therapy relationship is to make it no longer necessary.

A social worker colleague, Jim Lantz, once said to me: "The whole of life is captured metaphorically in the first few seconds after birth. The baby is cast out from the warmth and symbiosis with the mother during the birth process. Within seconds, the child is placed back upon the mother's belly. This, in an emotional sense, is the story of the rest of our lives: negotiating our separateness and connection to others."

Yes!

Chapter 7

TRUTHS AND FICTIONS

The word metaphor is derived from the Greek *meta,* meaning above or beyond, and phorein, meaning to carry from one place to another (Kopp, R. R., 1995); the latter is the same root as *amphora,* an ancient Greek vessel for carrying and storing precious liquids. Metaphors in language are also carriers: They hold information that hides meaning in symbolic form (B. L. Moon, 2007).

I have often thought that what my clients have most wanted from me as they made their way along the art therapy pilgrimage was an assurance that the truths about their lives are acceptable. To understand this idea, one must examine the concept of truth. In the rock opera *Jesus Christ Superstar* (Webber & Rice, 1970), Pilate sings/screams to Jesus: "But what is truth? Is truth unchanging law? We both have truths—are mine the same as yours?" This question, are my truths the same as yours, is at the root of many emotional and psychological struggles. For our purposes, truth is defined as sincerity in character and action: the sum of real things and events.

Most clients I have treated have suffered from the existential reality that many of the truths about their lives have been at best dysfunctional and at worst horrific. In response to the cognitive and emotional dissonance and pain of their lives, they have created fictional personas to ease their distress. These fictions are of course creative acts, and as such are metaphoric self-portraits and truths in their own rights.

An example of such fictionalizing was seen in the case of Anthony, a 22-year-old man I worked with at a residential treatment facility. After his mother abandoned Anthony as a child, he lived with a succession of extended family members who were physically and emotionally abusive. He ran away when he was 16, lived on the street, and got involved in a variety of nefarious activities. After multiple arrests, he was ordered into the treatment facility by the court. When I began to see him in art therapy, he had concocted a life story in which he was a heroic figure. He would often draw scenes from his life that my colleagues on the treatment team assured me were fabrications.

The team urged me to confront Anthony's "trumped-up stories," but I resisted. I believed that there was often a grain of truth in his stories, and I remembered my mentor, Jones, teaching me that the feelings of a drawing are always true whether or not the drawing is historically accurate.

Over time, I saw that Anthony's stories were metaphoric communications conveying both the pain he had endured and courage he'd manifested as he made his way in the world, ostensibly without the benefit of nurturance and support. The hero stories, although factually untrue, were emotionally authentic.

One task of art therapists is to listen to, see, and share stories through action. By encouraging our clients to make art and engaging in our own art practice, we work with, play with, and enact salient themes of clients' therapeutic passage. A critical responsibility is to see and respond to the truths that emerge as we share artistic processes and products. Sometimes, we hardly need to talk at all.

The use of metaphor is essential to the healing capacity of art therapists. The metaphors of art therapists are not exclusively spoken. In art therapy, metaphors are communicated in actions, sounds, and objects by which one thing (the client) is described in terms of another (art processes and products). The metaphors of art therapy have potential for multiple interpretations; their purpose is to illuminate or expose truth.

By nature, art therapists are metaphoreticians. It is our job to interact with and respond to graphic and symbolic images, language, and actions of our clients. By doing so, we convey that we are trying to understand the unspeakable messages that images, sounds, and behaviors express. Artistic activity helps clients give visible form to the metaphoric themes of their lives within the therapy milieu. Transformation of essential truths through creative action is what rituals have done within religious communities for centuries.

The rituals that clients and I engage in are the sacraments of the creative process. The preparation of the art therapy studio, gathering of materials, and arranging of tables, chairs, and easels are the initial actions of the rites that move from within the heart and soul of the client through the brush and onto the canvas. The themes of these ceremonial pursuits emerge as the client's inward journey unfolds. As I stand before a client's artwork, I am reverent, awed by the courage manifested as the truths and fictions of their lives are portrayed.

I believe that drawings, paintings, poems, performances, and sculptures are depictions of life, illustrations of reality. Each jagged line, vivid form, and chiseled crevice proclaim to the beholder, "I am here, and this is a truth about me!"

Every time a client scrawls brilliant red chalk across a page, dips a brush in tempera, and moves from palette to canvas, the client announces, "I am." As I struggle to comprehend these proclamations, I seek dialogue. I listen to the whole communication and, at every turn, resist the seductive pull to analyze, dissect, or label.

Openness to the client's artistic work promotes an atmosphere of contagious excitement involving self-exploration and self-discovery. As clients paint or draw in my presence, I am attentive to my relationship to the art. I believe that my response to their efforts impacts the therapeutic work. It is also essential that I actively engage in my own artistic process during these times. My willingness to tell my tale through imagery in the company of the client sets the stage for the sharing of truths and metaphoric fictions that are the foundation of all art therapy endeavors. Engaging in art processes in the course of the therapeutic encounters with clients is vital to pragmatic and ethical art therapy practice. The courage that I honor as I struggle with my own imagery is infectious. It helps establish a safe milieu in which clients are encouraged to enter their process of self-exploration. As clients' work begins, expressions trickle, ooze, gush, spew, and surge onto the page. Willingness to be with my own images lays the groundwork that allows clients to believe that I might be able to understand their expressions. When I can open myself to what has been expressed, clients experience the double edge of therapeutic benefit: the cathartic relief of emotional expression and awareness that another has understood them.

The Gargoyle and Estelle

As I was writing a progress note in a client's medical chart early one morning, a nurse placed a piece of folded-up notebook paper on the table in front of me. "Look at this!" she said. "This is a really sick one."

I unfolded the paper and saw a grotesque pencil drawing of a human figure. Although the image was disturbing and malevolent, the artist clearly possessed better than average skills, as evidenced by line character, shading techniques, and attention to detail. The nurse explained that the drawing was found in the coat pocket of a young woman who had been an emergency admission to the adolescent unit the night before. She said that the client, Estelle, had caused a commotion when she was brought onto the unit. She had been combative and self-destructive, severely bitten her wrist, and required restraints for the night. The nurse added that Estelle had howled for several hours disturbing everyone's sleep. "So what do you make of this?" she asked.

I replied, "Well, it's hard to look at, but she does have a good touch with pencils. I look forward to meeting her when she's ready to be out on the unit or in activities."

"It may be awhile," the nurse muttered.

I could tell from her tone that my colleague was uncomfortable with the drawing. Estelle's behavior had clearly disrupted the tranquility of the unit, and the drawing was seen as an indicator of pathology, and threat to the security and predictability of the unit. This brief interaction between the nurse and me illustrates a tension that often exists between art therapists and members of other treatment disciplines in inpatient settings. It is the role of art therapists to value and honor artistic expressions of clients, even when such expressions seem primitive or disturbing. In contrast, nursing personnel are charged with maintaining a calm and predictable milieu. While I found Estelle's drawing both bizarre and intriguing, my nurse colleague saw it as potentially disruptive.

I was walking through the unit one afternoon a few days later when my attention was caught by a small frail woman sitting at one of the large round tables in the cafeteria. She was bent over a sketchpad working intently. I approached her.

"Hello, my name is Bruce," I said.

She did not lift her eyes from the page but said, "Are you the art guy they told me about?"

I was surprised and said, "Yes, how did you know that?"

She continued to draw and said: "Some of the other girls told me about the adolescent art therapy studio. They described you pretty good. Besides, you are the only guy with a gray beard, and no suit and tie."

"You are very observant," I said. "That's a good skill to have if you like art."

"I love art," she said. "If I don't die, I might want to be an artist."

"Do you mind if I look at what you are drawing?" I asked.

She did not answer but pushed the sketchpad across the table toward me. The drawing was of a nude woman fastened to the ground by spikes. Several man-beasts surrounded the woman with their hands covering their genitals. The image was provocative and cruel, but well rendered. I sensed tension as she watched me look at her work, perhaps expecting me to be repulsed or respond in a punitive way. I did neither.

I commented: "You know, the torso of this woman seems a bit out of proportion. Either it is too small or the head is too large. Did you mean to distort the figure?"

She replied, "I want the head to be big because of all the stuff that goes on in my head."

"In that case, you've really done a nice job of presenting a painful and troubling idea," I said. "By the way, as I said, my name is Bruce."

For the first time she looked up at me through the strands of hair that fell across her eyes. "I'm Estelle," she said.

I sat down in the chair across the table from her. "It's nice to meet you, Estelle," I said.

She half-smiled and said, "It's nice to have somebody look at my drawings without cringing."

"What do you mean?" I asked.

She stared at her hands and said, "The staff says that I have to close my sketchbook whenever other kids come around. I can tell they don't like my drawings."

I thought for a moment and replied: "You have good drawing skills. Do you always work in pencil?"

"Yeah," she said. "That's all I ever had at home."

"How about at school?" I asked.

"I've been in SBH (Severe Behaviorally Handicapped) since third grade, and they didn't have art classes," she said.

"How did you develop your techniques then?" I asked.

Estelle offered a wry smile and said: "There was a Michelangelo book in the library at school. I'd check it out and try to copy. I bet I've had that book out a hundred times."

"Well, Estelle, I have to get to a meeting," I said. "I hope that you'll get out to the studio for adolescent art soon. I'd love to teach you to paint." She said nothing, but as I walked toward the door, I felt her eyes on my back.

A few days later, I was informed that Estelle would be joining the morning studio art session. Her treatment plan listed three goals for the studio art experience: (1) Develop a more positive view of self through mastery of task; (2) enhance artistic and verbal expressive skills; and (3) promote a therapeutic alliance through shared tasks.

She stood in the doorway of the studio, with her arms folded across her chest, head down, and hair falling in an unkempt mane over her eyes. Frank, the staff member who had escorted her to the creative arts building, said: "Mr. Moon, this is Estelle. This is her first day off the unit." He whispered to me, "Do you want me to stay here with her; she is a wild one!"

I shook my head and said: "No, Frank, that won't be necessary. I've met Estelle before, and I think things will be okay." I turned to her and said: "Do you remember me, Estelle? I met you the other day on the unit. You showed me one of your drawings."

She looked up and said, "You changed your clothes." Then her eyes began to take in the studio.

In that facility, my colleagues and I tried to have as much art as we could hang on the walls. We wanted to create an environment that was stimulating to the creative urges of our clients. We hung current client works, some of our own paintings and drawings, and works that had been left by former clients. The effect was chaotic, resourceful, and contagious. At times, the space appeared cluttered and messy, but we believed that an infectious tone was set for the creative process because the studio was always in a state of reorganization and structuring. In a wonderful sense, the studio was an inanimate symbol of the role of the arts in therapeutic work, including the endless process of making sense out of chaos, and finding order in disorder.

"Estelle," I said, "let me give you a tour of the building." She followed me as I walked her through the various rooms of the creative arts building. As we re-entered the drawing and painting studio, I asked Estelle if she had any idea of what she'd like to work on.

She shrugged and asked, "Could I use some of that big paper and those drawing pencils you showed me?"

"Sure," I replied. I helped her gather a large sheet of drawing paper and a set of pencils with varying hardness. She chose to work at a table close to one of the corners of the room and sat with her back to the corner so that she could see everything around her. As she settled in, I asked: "Do you have any ideas about what you are going to draw? We like to have people working on themes that are important to them here in the studio."

She replied, "I'm going to draw what I always draw: the man."

"All right," I said. "I'll be over there working on my painting. Let me know if you need anything. Welcome to the studio, Estelle."

Saying no more, she got to work immediately. Although I worked on my painting, I watched her progress. Estelle's style of drawing was unlike any that I'd encountered. She began by drawing one gnarled and spiky hand. She did not sketch the whole figure or even the entire hand. Rather, she worked meticulously, one detail at a time. She rendered the thumb, then moved to the index finger, then the middle finger, and onto the ring finger. In each instance, she completed her drawing of the appendage entirely. Care and attention was given to the wrinkles of the hand, crevices, and contours, as well as to the shadows and highlights. It was as if she could see the finished drawing in its fullness in her mind's eye. It was as if she was a stenographer taking dictation from some unseen imaginal source.

By the end of her first session, she had completed one hand, one wrist, and half a forearm. In later sessions, she continued to work on her drawing. She seldom spoke to her peers in the group. She would, however, routinely make contact with me as she entered the studio by asking where the pencils were. Obviously she knew where the pencils were, but this ritual served as her transition into the creative space. This ritual became the subject of playful cajoling among other clients. One would ask, "Where are the paintbrushes?" Another would ask, "Where are the paper towels today?" If Estelle noticed these impersonations, she didn't respond in an observable manner. I suspect that she was aware of these and derived some sense of acceptance and pleasure as her peers imitated her interactions with me. It was my hunch that Estelle had often been the brunt of teasing and ridicule in her life, and to have her peers impersonate her in a warm spirited manner must have been a delightful change. Had I sensed any cruelty in the mimicry, I would have interceded. This, however, had a different feeling. Estelle's peers had stumbled upon a way to relate to her that she was willing to tolerate.

As the sessions progressed, the figure of a misshapen gargoyle emerged on the page. Portrayed in harsh light, his muscles rippled and his distorted face cast deep shadows across a hairy chest. It was a discomforting portrait.

As Estelle finished the right wrist, she beckoned me to her place in the room. As I approached, she said, "Something is wrong." She looked furtively toward the gargoyle.

"What do you mean?" I asked.

She brought a hand to her face and shook her head. "I can't see what is in his hand," she said.

"Oh, I know that feeling," I said. "Sometimes I feel like the whole canvas is staring at me just waiting for me to do something, only I can't figure out what it is I supposed to do."

"But this never happens to me, Bruce!" she said.

"Estelle, it happens to every artist," I said. "You can either try to fight your way through it, or sit back and wait awhile. Either way, something always comes."

She took her hand away from her face and asked, "Do you really believe that?"

"I have a lot of faith in the creative process," I said. "I have learned to trust it."

She asked, "How could I fight through this?"

"Well, one way is to do some study sketches and try out different options," I said. "Another way is to ask other people what they think should come next."

She seemed interested in the latter idea. "Do you ever get ideas that you use from other people?" she asked.

"Sure," I said. "And sometimes their ideas spark new ones of my own. It's really just a way to get a different perspective on my work."

She pulled her hair away from her eyes and asked, "So what would you put in the right hand?"

"Hmmm, I think I see a rock, like a rough and jagged piece of quartz or something like that," I said.

She frowned and said, "I don't know."

"Well, Estelle, there are other people in the room whom you could ask," I said.

She turned toward a boy who was working at the next table and asked, "Tony, what do you think should be in my man's right hand?"

He stood up to get a better look at the drawing and said: "I don't know. If it were me, I'd probably want it to hold a bag of weed."

Estelle rolled her eyes and looked over at me as if to say, "What a stupid idea this is."

"Try again," I prodded.

"Hanna, what do you think I should add to this drawing?" Estelle asked.

Hanna came over and stood behind Estelle. "He sort of reminds me of that guy on *Beauty and the Beast*. Why don't you put yourself in the picture holding hands with the monster?"

A stunned look came over Estelle's face. She did not respond.

"Did I say something wrong?" Hanna asked. "I didn't mean to . . ."

"It's ok, Hanna," I assured her. "Why don't you go back to your work." Estelle said no more for the rest of that session. In a mechanical fashion, she cleaned up, put her drawing away, and left the building. The following day was Friday; she refused to attend the session. The next Monday, she had a family therapy appointment that conflicted with her studio time, so I did not see her until the Tuesday after the events above.

She entered the room and asked, "Where are my pencils?"

"Hi Estelle," I replied. "They are over on the counter in the white basket."

"I brought some drawings with me for you to look at, Bruce," she said, putting her sketchbook on the table beside my easel. There were three drawings in the book. The first portrayed a toddler clasping the little finger of the right hand of a gargoyle. The second showed an older child with a balled-up fist resting in the open palm of a man. The third appeared to be a detailed self-portrait with Estelle's hand depicted gingerly holding the wrist of the right arm, with the palm of the gargoyle's hand open and bleeding.

"Yowsa!" I exclaimed. "These are not what I expected to see."

"They are what I see," Estelle said quietly.

"Which one are you going to use for your drawing?" I asked.

"I'm going to use them all," she replied.

"How do you mean?" I asked.

"I'm going to do three drawings altogether," she said. She gestured toward the drawing she'd been working on and added, "This one is for the baby."

Estelle finished her first drawing of the gargoyle. Then she copied the pose of the distorted figure twice more, adding the details described earlier. The result was a grotesque and tender triptych.

When she completed the three gargoyle drawings, she commenced to work on a piece of illustration board, approximately four feet square. As she stared at the empty panel, Hanna, now her roommate on the unit, said, "Why don't you draw him getting a haircut and shave?" This inspired laughter from Estelle's peers.

Estelle did not laugh. She threw her pencil to the floor and left the room, making her way to the bathroom down the hall. She did not return to the studio for the rest of session and refused to attend the next day.

The afternoon of the day she had refused to come to the studio, I happened to be passing through the unit. I saw her sitting alone in the music-listening area. I knocked on the glass door, and she waved me in. "Estelle, I missed you this morning in studio," I said.

"Yeah, I should have come," she sighed. "Hanna just pissed me off the other day, and I let it get to me."

"I was wondering about that," I said. "I thought maybe people were trying to make the beast into something he is not."

"Exactly!" Estelle said. "That's what I hate about that fairy tale. In the end, the beauty kisses the beast, and he turns into some handsome prince. Why couldn't anybody like him just the way he was?"

"Yes, I know what you mean, Estelle," I said. "I think a lot of people have trouble accepting things they see as ugly because it reminds them of parts of themselves."

Estelle's gargoyle was repeatedly portrayed the two months that she was in the hospital. Over time, his features softened, becoming less grotesque and frightening. He never became a handsome prince, but I believe that he was tamed as Estelle's creativity breathed life into his countenance. Parallel to the changes in the gargoyle were similar changes in Estelle. As she domesticated the beast, she gently tamed her own wildness.

Many of the historic realities of Estelle's life were dysfunctional and hurtful. In response to the pain, she created a gargoyle with the ugliness and hurt that she could not put into words. This creative act allowed her both to contain and express unspeakable feelings. Was the gargoyle real? No. Was his presence in her life a historic fact? No. But this fictional character was nevertheless an expression of truth.

Some thought that Estelle's drawings did nothing more than chronicle the work that she did in other therapeutic arenas. I assert that the progress she experienced in the psychiatrist's and social worker's offices was possible because of the creative metaphoric therapy that took place in the art therapy studio.

Chapter 8

FUNDAMENTAL PRINCIPLES
OF ART THERAPY

Members of my family and friends from other vocations have often asked me to define art therapy. It does not matter when I explain that I have written many books on the subject. They want to hear, in 30 seconds or less, what art therapy is. I cannot compress this chapter into 30 seconds. I can, however, distill over 30 years of clinical, supervisory, and educational experience in an attempt to examine what I consider to be the 10 fundamental principles of the field: (1) Art therapy is metaverbal; (2) talk can be a source of validation; (3) art therapy works with a wide range of populations; (4) creative actions in art therapy promote satisfaction and self-esteem; (5) artistic expression is healthy; (6) art therapy can be enhanced by imagination; (7) art therapy encourages clients to render emotional portraits of significant people and events in their lives; (8) art therapy lets clients make objects that represent feelings and thoughts; (9) original feelings related to events in the client's life stay attached to artistic portrayals; and (10) art therapists have two essential tools, art and self.

Principle One: Art Therapy is Metaverbal

The first, and perhaps most important, principle of art therapy is that our work goes beyond words. This means that the most important aspects of art therapy happen in the interaction among the client/artist, media, image, and artistic process. Art therapists' primary task is to provide an environment that facilitates these interactions.

The metaverbal nature of art therapy is easy to grasp in relation to clients' creative work in the art therapy studio. It is harder to understand in relation to individual and group art psychotherapy because of the verbal discussion that occurs in these contexts. When I stress the principle of metaverbal interaction in art therapy courses, students often question the validity of this tenet. My response to their challenge is consistent: I believe that the majority of work that takes place in an art psychotherapy group has been done before the client or I ever say a word about the image. Essentially, talking about the artwork is the icing on the cake. The main course of the therapeutic meal takes place among client, media, process, and product. The real substance of the art therapy sessions is beyond the capacity of spoken words. This is not a devaluation of verbalization, but rather an honoring of action and image. I have participated in many hours of art therapy work in which little or nothing was said, but much was done.

Principle Two: Talk Can Be a Source of Validation

In light of my description of the metaverbal nature of art therapy, one may wonder why art therapists would ever talk. The answer to that question is that humans are naturally talkative creatures. Talking about images, paintings, drawings, and other art forms offers psychological safety and security for both the client and therapist. For clients, the act of talking about artistic processes and products provides an opportunity to create emotional distance from the powerful feelings often evoked through the work. As clients use words to describe their artistic efforts, they shift from a sensual and emotional position toward acceptable cognitive explanations of the artwork. In some cases, this distancing can be helpful to clients. In other instances, it may be problematic.

In the case of a 17-year-old young woman with severe anxiety and features of Post-Traumatic Stress Disorder (PTSD), for example, it was helpful to encourage her to talk about pictures she made of the sexual abuse she had endured by her uncle. It was also soothing to her to be assured by the art therapist and peers in the group that children are in no position to ward off such inappropriate sexual behaviors on the part of adult authority figures. A member of the group explained, "It wasn't your fault, Sarah, and you are guilty of nothing. You have a right to be angry at him, but you should no longer be ashamed." These words offered the client comfort and consolation as she wrestled with demons from her history.

In contrast is the case of the mid-40s sales representative who came to the hospital seeking treatment for his depression. It quickly became clear that in addition to being depressed, he had been drinking excessively and was likely an alcoholic. He was a charming, yet subtly untrustworthy man. He was adept at using his words to keep himself a safe distance from others while also managing to be the life of the party.

In response to the drawing task in group, "Portray the animal in your head and the animal in your gut," he drew a collie for the head and a fearsome dragon in his belly. When it came his turn to share, he launched into a long entertaining monologue. He had everyone in the room laughing heartily. I said nothing. As his story wound down, I made eye contact with him. Without speaking, I shook my head slowly, side to side. The group, sensing an unspoken tension, quieted.

He looked at me and said, "What?"

I opened my mouth as if about to speak, but remained silent.

He raised his voice and snapped, "What's your problem?"

Intuiting that any effort I made to interact with him through talking would be an exercise in futility, I raised my right hand and gestured toward the drawing of the collie. I mimed petting the dog. With my left hand, I reached toward the trembling dragon. As one hand amiably stroked the air, the other shook with growing intensity. I looked from hand to hand, then at the client. His face reddened, and he said, "What is that bullshit all about?" He pointed toward my hands. "Is that supposed to mean something?" he asked.

I nodded.

He snorted: "This is a bunch of shit. I don't get it. I don't get any of it."

I quietly said, "I believe you."

Looking toward his peers with mixed annoyance and desperation, he jeered, "I'm lost, man."

Again, I said, "I believe you."

"What the hell are you talking about?" he asked.

I replied: "I believe you. I believe that you feel lost."

In this illustration, I used words sparingly only to validate the deep meanings expressed in the client's artwork. I felt little urge to talk during this interchange. It was apparent that, at a metaverbal level, the client had already begun to struggle with the incongruity of his tame and charming exterior, and the wild and frightening inner feelings characterized in the animal imagery. There was little need to talk.

I want to be clear about this point: The essential role of verbalization in art therapy is one of validation. The crucial work in the art therapy session takes place among the client/artist, media, and image in the presence of the art therapist.

Principle Three: Art Therapy Works with a Wide Range of Populations

Art therapy can be used with a range of clients from young to old. No one is excluded on the basis of gender or sexual orientation. The arts are multicultural, and art therapists work with people of many races, creeds, and religious traditions. Art therapy is effective with individuals, couples, families, and groups. It works equally well with the intellectually gifted and learning impaired. It can be effective for clients who are mentally ill, terminally ill, vision-impaired, or deaf.

Throughout history, wherever people have gathered to form communities, the arts have sprung to life. Similarly, wherever suffering people seek help, the arts emerge as a potent psychic balm. As members of a helping profession, art therapists often find themselves working with people with whom the rest of society is uncomfortable. Abused and angry children and adolescents, people suffering from life altering diseases, people facing the last stage of their lives, people who have serious multiple handicaps and developmental challenges, and the homeless, imprisoned, and hopeless. In short, art therapists often help people who have been marginalized and disenfranchised. In any circumstance focusing on human well-being, art therapists can positively contribute.

Principle Four: Creative Actions in Art Therapy Promote Satisfaction and Self-Esteem

I am often awed by the look in clients' eyes as they sign their work, stand back, and gaze at what they have done. It is as if the air in the studio is filled with the soundless proclamations by the artist, "I am!" This principle reminds me of the first sentence in Vonnegut's (1998) *Timequake,* "A plausible mission of artists is to make people appreciate being alive at least a little bit" (p. 1). I have worked with many clients who initially enter the therapeutic studio with an attitude of distrust. It is as if they do not believe that making art will help them, and as if their problems are too complicated or serious to be eased by what they sometimes regard as a frivolous activity.

I have been providing pro bono art therapy for several years at a residential treatment facility that specializes in working with adolescent boys who have committed a sexual offense. This is a difficult environment to live in and, because they were ordered into treatment by the court system, most of the clients are cautious when it comes to expressing feelings. Many of the residents, in addition to having committed a sexual offense, are themselves victims of sexual abuse. Therefore, while dealing with the emotional consequences of their offending behavior, the boys also struggle with their own victimization. These complex and painful emotions include low self-esteem, powerlessness, shame, guilt, fear, embarrassment, betrayal, and rage. Given the serious nature of past behaviors and the complexity of their emotional struggles, it is understandable that they are guarded and defensive, and incapable of engaging in insight-oriented psychotherapy with an adult authority figure. Yet I have found that after an initial period of resistance to art therapy, nearly all of the clients come to view the art therapy studio as a place of safety in which they learn to take pride in their artist expressions. For many of these clients, the gratification they received from their artistic endeavors is a new experience.

Principle Five: Artistic Expression Is Healthy

Jones, a pioneer of the art therapy profession, repeatedly emphasizes that we must treat a client's dysfunction by functioning with the client. A simplified illustration of this principle is found in the case of a severely depressed man who, prior to coming to the hospital, had retreated to his bed and refused all his life responsibilities. While the resident psychiatrist assigned to treat the man was captivated by the client's explanations of his disease, Jones would have insisted that the client participate in the morning physical-conditioning activity in the hospital gym. This was followed by an hour in the art therapy studio and regimen of other activities throughout the day. Unsurprisingly, the client reported feeling better by the afternoon of the second day that he participated in calisthenics, painting group, and other activities. It feels good to do things, especially to express feelings artistically.

We live in a culture that does not always value emotional expression. This is especially true for men, but women are not exempt from such pressures either. We are bombarded by influences that stress the virtues of stoicism and heroic figures are often "the strong silent type." In a host of ways, we are given the message that we should keep our feelings to ourselves, and that emotional expression is a sign of weakness. The result of this enculturation is a communal quality of undeveloped emotional life. Thus, the world is full of people who cannot, or will not, express their feelings verbally. The arts are a natural and healthy counterinfluence.

Principle Six: Art Therapy Can Be Enhanced by Imagination

Some clients may never be able to express their feelings in words. Reticence to talk may be the result of psychological, sociological, or biological influences, or all of these. Other clients derive benefits from talking about feelings that emerge in their artwork. Whether they can talk about feelings or not, it is often true that before clients' feelings can be put into words, issues arise and can be worked with by engaging imagination and fantasy through art-making.

A Penny for Your Thoughts

Penny's depression was profound and troubling. Her father reported that she had always been an outgoing and cheerful girl. She'd gotten good grades, participated in cheerleading, and was a popular and active adolescent. In fact, he said that since her mother died of cancer three years earlier, she had been "a real trooper." She had taken over caring for her younger brother and sister. She cleaned the house, cooked the meals, and organized the family's life as best she could. Over the summer, she gradually became less active. When school began in fall, Penny withdrew from her extracurricular activities. Her grades dropped significantly. Finally, late one Saturday evening, her father found her slumped in a chair in her bedroom. He tried to wake her, but she didn't respond. He immediately called the rescue squad, and she was taken to a local hospital where her stomach was pumped. She had taken a handful of sleeping pills.

The first few days of her hospitalization, Penny was listless. Although she cooperated with the treatment program, she did so in a passive manner as if she were just going through the motions. She didn't talk much. Her initial drawing in the art therapy group, however, spoke volumes. The art task I had assigned that day was to respond to the following guided image: Imagine that you've been walking in the woods. You come upon the mouth of a cave. For a moment, you consider walking past, but your curiosity won't allow it. Go into the cave to the deepest part. Look around yourself. What do you see? How does it smell? How does it feel in there?

Penny's drawing was of a large Winnie-the-Pooh-like bear standing in front of the cave opening. The mouth of the cave was dark and foreboding. A child was portrayed standing before the bear.

When it was her turn to share, she said: "I couldn't get into the cave. The bear wouldn't get out of my way!"

I responded, "It looks like a very big bear."

"Yes," Penny said. "He is big. He wasn't mean or anything like that, but he wouldn't move."

"This is a really interesting picture, Penny," I said. "Would you be willing to use your imagination and talk with me about it?"

She nodded.

"Good," I said. "Now, what I'd like for you to do, Penny, is pretend that you are Winnie the Pooh and that you can talk. I'll be the girl in the picture. What would you say to me?"

She closed her eyes momentarily and said: "I'd say, get out of here. This is no place for little girls."

"But I want to go in there and look around," I replied.

In a slightly more stern voice, Penny said: "Go home to your mother. This cave is dark, wet, and scary. You don't want to go in there."

"Oh, but I do," I said. "I want to explore."

The bear growled: "You have no business in there. If you go in, you may never come out again. Now go home to your mother like I told you to." As these words left her lips, Penny began to cry. She said nothing more that session.

The ensuing weeks of therapy explained the significance of Penny's first drawing. The depiction of Pooh, Penny, and the cave captured the essence of her therapy. The cave emerged as a representation of Penny's developmental need to separate herself from her family. One crucial task of adolescence is emancipation. Her mother's death had interrupted her process of separation and individuation. The cave may also have symbolized her need to experiment with sexuality and her struggle to understand her own interior depths. It certainly allegorized the adolescent psychic tasks of self-exploration.

The Pooh bear stood in her way representing obstacles in her path to individuation. Among these obstacles were her father, her younger siblings, and the absence of her mother. The message of the bear was, "Don't explore the dark and wet regions of yourself." In effect, it meant, "Don't grow up."

In the imaginal dialogue between Penny and the bear, which represented herself, the repeated comment by the bear, "go home to your mother," seemed important. One interpretation of this message could be that the only way past the obstacles to emancipation was to join her mother by committing suicide.

The drawing showed the guilt that Penny felt. Perhaps it stemmed from a preconscious sense that she had won the *Oedipal* battle. Her mother was dead, and she was now in the position of wife to her father. Compounding the guilt were feelings about her own longing for sexual contact with peers, anger at having been thrust into an adult role too early, and resentment toward her younger siblings.

Penny was not in the hospital long. The drawing provided the treatment team with keys to understanding the feelings that had precipitated her suicide attempt. Once these were understood, it was easy to begin to counter her unrealistic guilt with supportive reassurance that her feelings were natural. Family therapy helped lighten the expectations on Penny, and roles within the family unit were redefined to make her everyday tasks less burdensome. In many ways, the course of Penny's therapy was delineated by the images she created in the art therapy group.

Principle Seven: Art Therapy Encourages Clients to Render Emotional Portraits of Significant People and Events in their Lives

The potency of this principle was illustrated early in my career as I treated a woman named Helen. She entered the hospital with profound depression. Her husband had died unexpectedly a few months earlier. Since his death, she had gradually become less active, and withdrawn from her family and friends. After a time, Helen had almost ceased to function, choosing to isolate herself at home and do nothing.

The attending psychiatrist suspected that unresolved issues between

Helen and her late husband were blocking her ability to grieve. The problem for the treatment team was how to engage a dead man in the therapy work that Helen needed to do. The answer that emerged was that Helen would be encouraged to draw and paint images of her husband and their relationship. One such drawing portrayed Helen discovering the fallen body of her husband in their kitchen. As she finished, I saw tears well up in her eyes. When she began to speak of this drawing, however, the feelings connected to it were not sadness or loss. Helen was angry. Something about the way that she portrayed the scene had sparked the anger she felt toward her husband for deserting her.

Raising her voice, she addressed the picture: "How could you leave me here all alone? We were supposed to retire together, see the world, and live happily ever after. How dare you ruin everything!" As these words hung in the air, she cried.

In subsequent drawings, Helen created an artistic dialogue with her husband. She imagined what he would say to her and how she would respond. Through this process, she was able to symbolically resolve some of her feelings of abandonment, loss, and anger.

Principle Eight: Art Therapy Lets Clients Make Objects that Represent Feelings and Thoughts

The process of creating artworks affords both the client and art therapist something to dialogue with and about. Clients often find that talking about the characters or artistic elements in their artwork is less threatening than directly discussing feelings and treatment issues.

It is safe to assume that clients admitted to psychiatric hospitals have already tried to alleviate their emotional distress on an outpatient basis and typically have been involved in traditional verbal psychotherapy without significant relief. The same holds true for individuals who seek art therapy on an outpatient basis: They have usually engaged in other forms of therapy to no avail. The reasons for the failure of verbal psychotherapy are, of course, as numerous and varied as the clients themselves.

It is the creation of something objective, an art piece, that differentiates the work of art therapists from that of psychologists, social workers, psychiatrists, and counselors. The painting. sculpture, or drawing is the focal object, and it is during creation that the relationship between art therapist and client is constructed. The artwork provides both a subject and context for the therapist and client to be together in relationship. Sometimes the artwork is spoken about, and sometimes the client is asked to give the image a voice and speak from its perspective. Other times, there is no talking at all.

Rob's World

I first met Rob when he was referred to the art therapy studio. The instructions of the treatment team were to help Rob develop expressive skills. He was a hostile and crude 25-year-old. He'd been admitted to the hospital upon the recommendation of his lawyer because he was facing serious charges of assault and battery, and the lawyer hoped that a mental health evaluation could benefit his defense.

Rob was 6'4" and weighed 225 pounds. He was not pleased to be in the hospital, despite the fact that he had signed a voluntary admission agreement. Within a few hours in the hospital, he had established a pattern of relating in which he intimidated peers and staff. He was loud and vulgar.

He came to the art therapy studio his second day of hospitalization. He'd been in the building for only a few minutes when his obnoxious verbal devaluing began. He raised his voice and said: "This is ridiculous. Why in the hell do you want me play around with this bull?"

"Rob," I said, "I know that doing art is often something that people have not done for a long time when they come here. But, we think that it is a very healthy thing to do, and it might help us understand you better." I sensed that Rob's bravado was a cover for feelings of inadequacy and self-loathing. The volume level of his resistance seemed almost desperate, as if demanding attention and care.

He snarled, "So, wha'd'ya want me to do?"

I handed him a piece of Masonite, approximately 18" x 24" in size. "I'd like you to think about a rock," I said.

"Why should I think about a rock?" he asked.

"Well, you seem to be a really strong and solid guy," I said. "Maybe if you paint a picture of a rock, it will help me understand how you feel."

Rob replied, "I ain't got any feelings!"

I said, "Do you mean that you are numb, empty, or dead?"

"Huh?" he asked.

"Rob, to have no feelings at all, you either have to be numb, empty, or dead," I said. "Which are you?"

He slammed his meaty fist on the table. "I ain't none of that," he told me.

"All right, Rob," I said. "Let's back up. If you were a rock, what kind of rock would you be?"

He thought for a moment and said, "Coal!"

"Okay," I said. "I'd like you to begin by painting this Masonite panel like fire."

He gave me a puzzled glance and asked, "Why fire?"

"You seem pretty angry about things, Rob, so I thought of fire when you said coal," I said.

"So how do I start?" he asked. "I don't know how to make no fire."

I suggested that he place several blobs of orange, yellow, and red paint randomly on the panel. When he had done so, I showed him how to use a large brush in continuous long strokes to pull the paint across the board. I could tell by the look on his face that he was immediately gratified when the warm colors blended together as he drew the brush from left to right.

"Damn, this is all right," he said.

The next day, I asked Rob to imagine the shape of the coal that he wanted to paint.

He said, "I dunno, just coal-shaped."

"Well, how about taking a piece of notebook paper and crumpling it up so it's shaped like a rock?" I said.

Rob told me he'd try.

A few minutes later, he brought me a wadded piece of paper. I said: "Good job, Rob. It really looks like a piece of coal. Now try to draw it onto the board with a piece of chalk."

When he finished that task, I again praised his effort.

"Now what?" he asked.

I replied. "Now I want you to paint it pure black."

When he finished painting the coal shape black, he explained, "I thought there should be some lines or something to show the shape of the coal."

I suggested he use blue to indicate the edges and surfaces of the piece of coal.

When Rob finished his painting, he received several positive comments from his peers in the studio. He seemed genuinely surprised and pleased by their praise. It so happened that he was the last of the clients to leave the creative arts building that morning. I was at the sink cleaning some paintbrushes when he approached me. "You know, I never did paint anything before in my life–'cept the garage."

I looked up from the sink and said: "You did well, Rob. I like the painting a lot."

"I wanted to ask you something," he said. "I know that this sounds funny, but when I look at that thing I uh . . . " he began.

"It makes you feel something?" I said.

"Yeah, isn't that screwy?" he asked.

I dried my hands and said: "It happens all the time, Rob. I think that pictures sometimes know more about us than we do."

"What?" he asked, looking at me incredulously.

"Never mind," I said. "I wonder what that piece of coal would say if it had a voice?"

Rob laughed, then feigned a tortured scream.

"That doesn't sound angry," I said.

"It ain't angry," he said. "It's bein' burned up and that would hurt!"

Our work together was the first hint from Rob that there was more to him than the angry, macho facade he showed the world. Other paintings and sculptures followed. Images of his loneliness, self-loathing, and inadequacies emerged. He seldomly talked about his artworks, but they spoke for him eloquently. In rare moments, Rob put words to his art. However, when it was suggested directly that perhaps the feelings he associated with his pictures might be his own, he quickly retreated into his brutish style of interaction. As long as the image was the subject of conversation, he would try to stay with it. As soon as Rob himself became the focus, his bravado and bluster would return. Through his images, Rob was able to share feelings of emptiness, anger, and sadness. These aspects of self would never have been known had it not been for his art.

Principle Nine: Original Feelings Related to Events in the Client's Life Stay Attached to Artistic Portrayals

All artists know that artworks can call up intense feeling. When a drawing is created in an effort to represent an incident, regardless of how long ago the original event was, the feelings of that event are recalled with much the same power as they held at their occurrence.

Every so often, I rearrange the storage space in my studio. As I do, I am bombarded by image memories held in the paintings and drawings I come across. Each artwork is emotionally charged. On one level, I can recall the sensations of the scene: I smell the smells and hear the sounds. On another level, I can also recall the process of creating the work: I remember the period of my life that produced the piece, complete with pleasures and struggles.

The technical psychological term for this process is cathexis, which means investment of libidinal energy in a person, object, or idea. I have seen cathexis as clients portray painful experiences from their past. In the context of the art therapy session, it is as if clients and I enter a time machine and are transported back to the traumatic event. This provides both of us with an emotional window to the past. This is important to the therapeutic use of the arts because clients often experience difficulty relating to the past through verbal constructions. This is why art therapy has become a primary treatment modality for people with PTSD. Whether a client is suffering from the after effects of war, or physical, sexual, or emotional abuse, they come to treatment longing to resolve feelings related to the tragic past to live peacefully in their present. Artworks that remain cathected to traumatic events are key to understanding the experiences of the client. Similarly, the cathartic process of artistic expression offers clients an opportunity to purge destructive emotions and bring about the spiritual renewal that is integral to their recovery.

Principle 10: Art Therapists Have Two Essential Tools, Art and Self

The essential nature of art processes have been, and will continue to be, explored throughout this book. The use of self as a therapeutic tool is a vital concept. We art therapists must know ourselves before we attempt to deal with the lives of others. We cannot afford to have emotional blind spots that obscure our vision of the client. We must know ourselves well, and whenever possible, be at peace in our own being. It is impossible to be an effective therapist when one's life is in turmoil. I am not suggesting that art therapists should withdraw from the field at times of great personal stress. Rather, I believe that we must all be willing to work on ourselves. This means that at times in one's professional life, personal psychotherapy could be helpful.

Being an art therapist takes work. It requires the capacity to introspect and struggle with the images that emerge in one's own artworks. We should not be shy about seeking therapy, for this is an investment not only in our own well-being, but in the well-being of our clients. We must be willing to grapple with our own motivations, fantasies, and desires which led us to this profession. This means coming face-to-face with our strengths, weaknesses, virtues, and evils. We must wrestle with our omnipotent longings as they bump against our impotent realities. We must realize that as art therapists, we are only catalysts for change in the client's life. We cannot force clients to be healthy, for that is their responsibility.

I encourage all students and colleagues to participate in psychotherapy. This can do no harm but do much good. According to the proverb, "Physician, heal thyself." I urge art therapists to know themselves, as well.

Chapter 9

ART THERAPISTS AND
SOCIAL RESPONSIBILITY

I believe that art therapists have a social responsibility to the world. It is not enough to learn techniques and practice them in isolation from the society in which we live. Because of the tradition of artistic struggle passed to us from artists throughout history, as well as our corporate concern for the well-being of humanity, we are compelled to be active agents for change.

According to Fromm (1955):

Man today is confronted with the most fundamental choice . . . between robotism (of both capitalist and communist variety) or Humanistic Communitarian Socialism. Most facts seem to indicate that he is choosing robotism and that means, in the long run, insanity and destruction. But all these facts are not strong enough to destroy faith in man's reason, good will and sanity. As long as we can think of alternatives, we are not lost. As long as we can consult together and plan together, we can hope. But indeed, the shadows are lengthening, the voices are becoming louder. (p. 315)

I am reminded of some of the social sounds that I have heard these past four decades. Listen:

The war to end all wars came to a close.
The Korean War followed.
The Vietnam War followed.
The Gulf War followed.
The War in Afghanistan and Iraq War followed.
Martin Luther King proclaimed," I have a dream."

Other voices shouted," America, love it or leave it."
Shots echoed in the streets of Dallas.
Shots echoed in the streets of Memphis.
Shots echoed in the streets of Los Angeles.
President Nixon saw the light at the end of the tunnel.
The Beatles sang, All you need is love.
Mayor Daley demanded order in Chicago.
Governor Rhodes ordered National Guard troops onto the Kent State University
campus.
Draft cards burned.
Gloria Steinem gave us a new image of women.
President Carter announced there was malaise among the people.
It felt good if we did it.
Yuppies flourished.
We learned to drink Perrier.
President Reagan decried, that Evil Empire.
The bulls thundered, and the bears roared.
We were offered the image of a thousand points of light.
There would be no new taxes.
The Berlin Wall crumbled.
The Soviet Union tumbled.
The national debt skyrocketed.
The twin towers fell,
and on and on and on.

Our culture today does not value pain. Television commercials assure us that pain is unnecessary. All you need to do is take something to get rid of it, and pharmaceutical advertising suggests that almost everything has a cure or Band-Aid. We like things to be this easy. We like disposable things because they are easy: Use them then throw them away because who has time to recycle? We like easy relationships, easy sex, easy fast food, easy abortion, easy divorce, easy entertainment, and easy work. We like to take life easy, and we hope for an easy death.

If you enjoy dark comedy, you may like the underarm deodorant campaign that said, "Never let 'em see you sweat." It takes no great psychoanalytical thinking to interpret the common message of both pain relievers and deodorant commercials: "Don't put up with discomfort, and at all costs, don't let anyone know how you really feel."

In the hospital setting, I have seen disturbed people who were lost find themselves again. I have seen people in excruciating pain cease their running, and turn to face and tame their monsters. I have seen people who once lived only for the pleasures of the moment learn the deep joy of struggle. These accomplishments were made by doing art, not finding quick-fix solutions.

The studio, be it a music practice room, dance floor, stage, or room filled with empty canvases, can be a sanctuary: an emotional asylum. The studio protects the virtue of struggle and the value of pain. There, attempts are made, failures are allowed, mastery is accomplished through repetition of process, gratification is delayed, and successes are celebrated. In the studio, present day artists connect to the collective past of all artists who have come before them. It is from the sum of all works of art, the tradition, that artists make creative leaps and take their place in the long chain of art history.

Making art is like the process of giving birth. Art-making is an act of love, labor, and pain. The history of art is a saga of struggle, and because of this tradition, we art therapists are called to impact society by taking every opportunity to remind people that it is okay to hurt; that it is good to struggle; and that life is hard. Just as I believe that art therapists should define themselves by what they are rather than what they are not, clients should also come to terms with truths. Artists have responded to public tragedies throughout the ages, and in some cases, only works of art remain to remind us of a particular event. Art therapists have a responsibility to speak out creatively—to *art* out—our witness, protestations, and concerns about life.

ART AND PROTEST

We Westerners have become comfortable with the portraits of self that are created in the darkrooms of the studio photographer. Pleasant backdrops, filtered lenses, warm light, and retouching techniques provide us with pictures of the selves we wish we were: No pimples, no scars, no wrinkles (B. L. Moon, 1995). But artists attempt to express the realities of life that often include imperfections, flaws, and feelings and ideas that are not comfortable.

Recently I entered two paintings in the faculty biennial exhibition at Mount Mary College. *Drunk and Ready for War* (Figure 11) features a bottle of oil resting on an American Flag. *We Are Being Lied To* (Figure 12) holds the simple words of the title in a black background. Initially,

Figure 11. *Drunk and Ready for War*–Acrylic on canvas.

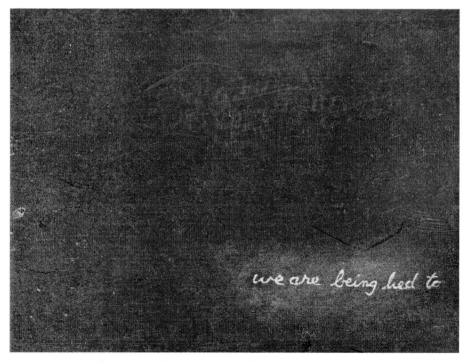

Figure 12. *We are Being Lied To*–Acrylic on canvas.

I was worried about submitting these pieces to the exhibition. I feared that my colleagues would see these paintings as too political or as anti-American. I received nothing but positive support from my coworkers. As a senior faculty member said, "It's about time somebody spoke up about these issues." These paintings are my art, my therapy, and one form of social action.

We live in a society that rewards political and corporate hoodlums—leaders who indirectly and directly pillage the earth's resources and look out for the interests of the wealthy—while inflicting the poor and powerless to random brutality in the name of patriotic capitalism. Art therapists have a responsibility to *art out* our witness, protestations, and concerns.

Where does all of this lead us? Art making is powerful and good and we need faith in this powerful goodness. Making art helps us bear the sadness, express the rage, protest the injustice, question the authorities, and celebrate the profound and the simple aspects of being alive. Art, like love, does not make us blind; rather, art enables us to see true colors.

Chapter 10

CURATIVE ASPECTS OF ART THERAPY

How does art therapy help clients? This is, in some ways, a naive question. Yet, if it can be answered with any sense of certainty, the art therapy profession will have a critical coordinate from which to map its approach to therapy. If we can observe, identify, and describe the essential roles that art plays in the process of facilitating therapeutic change, a logical foundation will form from which art therapists may construct treatment plans and philosophies.

The course of change in therapy is an intricate and difficult process. Change happens in the context of a complex weaving of relationship and experience. In the art therapy milieu, many relationships co-exist: client to therapist, materials, tools, images, and artworks, and therapist to client, materials, tools, images, and artworks. Likewise, multiple experiences, such as tactile, visual, and procedural ones, simultaneously occur in art therapy. The intersections of relationships and experiences are where the curative aspects of art therapy are enacted.

If a carpenter describes to a layman the entire process of building a house, the discourse can be overwhelmingly technical. However, if the carpenter only explains the function of 2 x 4s in the construction of walls, the description will be easier to understand. When discussing a complicated topic, it is helpful to first explore the simplest building blocks that create the whole. Following this logic, I will discuss the curative aspects of art in therapy by breaking them down into 12 categories: (1) art as existentialism; (2) art as communication; (3) art as soul; (4) art as mastery; (5) art as personal metaphor; (6) art as empowerment; (7) art as work; (8) art as play; (9) art as relationship; (10) art as structure and chaos; (11) art as hope; and (12) art as benevolence.

The following clinical illustrations of curative aspects of art therapy are intended to bring the reader into the art therapy studio to share a sense of the sounds and smells of these places, and the tastes of the interactions. To strengthen my descriptions of what makes art healing, I have consulted experts, colleagues, clients, and graduate students I have known over the past three decades.

Curative Aspect One: Art as Existentialism

Art psychotherapy is difficult. Usually it starts when the client is in the midst of a painful, disturbing, or frightening life crisis. The particular events and circumstances that lead a person to seek art therapy are as varied as the individuals themselves. However, common threads repeatedly appear. Existential therapists believe the primary dynamics that lead clients to therapy are the ultimate concerns of existence: freedom, aloneness, guilt, personal responsibility for one's own life, the inevitability of suffering and death, and a longing for purpose and meaning.

Existential art therapists focus their work on addressing client's anxieties and defense mechanisms that form in response to the ultimate concerns of life. They view their work as tied to creative struggles, and the core issues of meaning, isolation, freedom, and death (Figure 13).

Figure 13. *Finding Meaning*–Oil on canvas by Catherine Moon.

Artists have always known that a primary source of their creative work is their own emotional turmoil stimulated by struggles with the ultimate concerns. In existential therapy, people relate to these issues either by attempting to ignore them or living in what Yalom (1980) refers to as "a state of mindfulness." The client's awareness of the capacity to be self-creative in a state of mindfulness promotes the ability to change. Arts processes are natural activities for expression, which ultimately leads to mindfulness.

My work as an existential art therapist can be conceptualized as going on a pilgrimage with the client. To discover the meanings of the client's life as shown through artistic processes and products, I guard against temptations to become an interpreter or diagnostician, and encourage clients to make their own interpretations, acting as both analyst and analysand.

Throughout history, the arts have often dealt with the ultimate concerns of existence. This artistic tradition of grappling with the depths of human experience is an extraordinary gift of the artist therapist to clinical milieus. Artists have always struggled with issues of meaning, isolation, death, and creative freedom. As art therapists, we must also wrestle with the ultimate concerns of existence in the company of our fellow travelers because making art is a process of dealing with existential concerns.

In existential art therapy, art therapists focus on the art processes and products that emerge in the context of relationships with clients; thus, the essence of existential art therapy is found in clients' artworks. Working from this perspective, art therapists attend to clients by doing with them; being open to them; and honoring their pain (B. L. Moon, 1990, 1995). The primary thrust of the work is engaging the client in a creative struggle with the ultimate concerns of human existence. A central concept in using the arts therapies from an existential base is that the art processes lead individuals toward a state of mindfulness, which leads to creative anxiety, which leads to action and change, which fosters expression that deepens mindfulness; the method is circular.

Julie's Rocks

When Julie entered the short-term treatment unit at Harding Hospital, she was a recent graduate from a prestigious college. She was

23 years old, intelligent, and ambitious, but by her account, chronically depressed. She shared with her primary therapist that she had not felt happy since junior high. "The real lows don't come very often, but I just never feel good," she said.

Julie had been in the art therapy group for two sessions when she drew an image of two rocks that would become a recurring image for her. Initially, they were portrayed as elements of a tranquil but bleak landscape. Over a number of sessions, she drew several versions of the rocks. They were usually drawn with black and brown chalk, and typically one was tall and slender, while the other was a roughly circular shape. They were always leaning against each other. When asked about them, Julie would shake her head and say, "I don't have a clue why they are here; they just are."

On one such occasion, I responded to Julie by sharing a thought from Hillman's (1989) *A Blue Fire* that images are necessary angels waiting for our response.

"What do you think he meant by that?" Julie asked.

"Well, I'm not exactly sure how Hillman would answer your question, but I think he's talking about how sometimes images come to us because they have something to say or teach us."

She looked dubious and replied, "Hmmm, maybe they are telling me that I should lose some weight."

Her comment brought a round of laughter from her peers in the group.

"They do look heavy," I said. Addressing group members, I asked, "If anyone in the group was out walking and came upon these rocks, what would your reaction be?"

Bill, a man in his early sixties, said: "I think they look like a good place to rest. I'd sit on the smaller one and lean back on the tall one."

Jennifer, another recent college graduate, chimed in, "I think one is a guy rock, and the other one is a girl."

Marianne, a widow in her mid 30s said: "They look sort of lonely or lost to me. They keep showing up in your drawings, Julie, but it's like they don't know where they belong."

Immediately, Julie's facial expression went from a partial smile to ashen solemnity. Sensing the power of the necessary angels message, I asked Julie if she wanted to say anything more about her drawing.

She shook her head and quietly said, "No."

The next session, Julie's rocks again appeared. This time, they were depicted as if they were seated on a plush velvet love seat. The room containing them was portrayed as ornate, yet cold and uninviting. When it came her turn to speak, Julie said: "I've been doing a lot of thinking about these rocks. If they are angels, they are mean."

"Julie, sometimes the messages that we most need to hear are the ones we least want to listen to," I replied.

"Yes, I know," she said. "I don't like what the rocks have to say to me." Tears welled in her eyes.

Marianne asked, "What do you think they mean, Julie?"

"I'm not sure, but the other night I was thinking about them, and the faces of my mom and dad came to my mind," she said. "They were smiling at me, telling me how proud they are of me and what a good daughter I am, and what a great person I am." Tears ran down her cheeks and splattered on her blouse.

Bill said: "That sounds pretty good, Julie. What's the matter with that?"

Sobbing, she said: "It's not true, Bill, it's not true." Through her tears, Julie shared with the group that she had gotten pregnant when she was in high school. She and her boyfriend had decided that she should have an abortion. She kept both the pregnancy and abortion secret from her parents ever since.

Jennifer reached over and placed an arm around Julie's shoulders. "It's all right, Jul, it's all right," she said.

"No, no it's not!" Julie said. "It's all a lie. They think I'm Miss Perfect, and I feel horrible. I thought I'd forgotten all about it until those damned rocks showed up."

I said: "Maybe the rocks didn't want things to be forgotten. Maybe they need the truth to be told. They look pretty solid. I don't think they will crumble."

Julie attended three more expressive group sessions. The rocks came too. The dialogue between them encircled existential themes of guilt, loneliness, vulnerability, and forgiveness. During her final session, Jennifer asked Julie if she was going to tell her parents about the abortion. "I don't know yet," she replied. "But I do know that I have to make a decision about this. I can't just let it slide anymore; the rocks will get in the way."

Nearly four years after Julie left therapy, I received a letter from her. She included a photograph of herself, her husband, and their infant son. They were standing in front of a cluster of large rocks along the New England shoreline. The letter was, for the most part, newsy, catching me up on the twists and turns of her life post-treatment. She added a P.S.: "Everyone knows. The rocks survived."

Curative Aspect Two: Art as Communication

Every time a painter fills the brush and moves it across the canvas; every time an author pounds the keyboard; every time a poet scrawls a stanza; and every time a trumpeter wets lips and blows; a proclamation is made to the world: "I am here, I have something to say, and I am." As the audience beholds this, it honors the tired muscles, hours of practice, and deep feelings that have conspired to create.

In the art therapy studio, drawings, collages, sculptures, assemblages, and paintings provide the client and therapist with snapshots of inner life. Each line, shape, and color is a piece of reality that defies verbal description.

The etiology of words suggests that all language was once expressive and imaginative. However, clearly both spoken and written word have lost their original power. For many people, parallel to the phenomenon of the weakening of words has been a diminishment in meaningful use of their imaginative and creative capacities. Add to this a cultural trend toward avoidance of feelings, reflection, and sharing, and one is left with a client population with limited contact with authentic self-expression and self-exploration.

For many clients, therapeutic arts offer an authentic mode of communication sorely lacking in their lives. As clients paint in my presence, I am aware of their relationship to the processes, materials, and images that emerge. With each brush stroke, clients tell their tales, setting the stage for the sharing of stories that is the basis of the art therapy pilgrimage. These communications are often raw and painful, but always encouraging to me. As art therapists, we must be open to understanding whatever has been expressed. In so doing, we help establish a safe milieu in which clients/artists may engage in self-exploration. Art is communication. As clients paint, each line, shape, and color is a fragment of who they are. As the brush moves across the canvas, stories of selfhood are told, sometimes eloquently and sometimes painfully raw.

David and the Dark

David shuffled into the studio, eyes downcast and hair disheveled. Although it was a typical damp and cold February day in Ohio, he wore his slippers on the walk from the cottage to the art therapy studio. He was a tall, 37-year-old man, but he looked older. His face was creased with lines which, if read between, told stories of hard times.

I gave him a brief tour of the building and explained that we use the studio as a place to creatively work on important treatment issues. He said, "I can't paint."

I've found that often people share what they most need to share unconsciously in the first few moments of therapeutic encounters. Operating from this theory, I suggested that I teach him how to paint. He shook his head but seemed to lack the energy to resist more vociferously. The rest of that first session was spent building a frame, and stretching and gessoing canvas.

The next day, David and I talked about possible themes for his first painting. He said that he had no idea what to do. I asked, "If you tried to describe the way you've been feeling, what sort of words would you use?"

"They say that I'm depressed," he said with a sigh.

"David," I replied. "I'm not interested in what anyone else has told you about how you feel. How would you describe yourself?"

He thought for a moment and said, "Dark."

"Like the night or like in a cave?" I asked.

"It's like being in the woods at night," he said. "I can't run, and I can't see."

"Yowsa, what a great image!" I exclaimed. "How about we paint your night woods?"

"I told you before, Bruce, I can't paint," he said. "I don't know where I'd begin."

"Trust me," I said. "I think you should start by mixing up some midnight blue. We'll need a lot of it."

"How do I do that?" he asked.

I gathered jars of ultramarine blue, raw umber, black, and cobalt blue, and told David to experiment on a piece of palette paper. I also gave him a container and told him that when he gets the color he wants, he should mix enough to fill the container.

About 15 minutes later, David approached me with a full container of deep blue. "Now what?" he asked.

"Step one David is to cover your entire canvas with the dark," I said.

"The whole thing?" he asked.

'The whole thing," I replied. "You see, I think it's best to get rid of the white emptiness as soon as possible."

When that was done, we talked about a path, trees, and rocks that he imagined would be in the woods. (I thought it was encouraging that his first image was of a path; this suggested a sense of hope and direction.)

Using the midnight blue as a base color, David added burnt sienna and arrived at the shade he wanted for the path. From there, he altered his dark blue with burnt umber for tree trunks; hooker green and a touch of white for leaves; and grays for rocks.

David's handling of color became the object of conversation in the studio. Fellow clients and therapists alike would stop to comment on his subtle variations on dark blue. The painting grew into a study of dim shapes half hidden by the somber and haunting night air of the forest. From 15 feet away, the painting appeared to be nothing more than shadows. At closer range, it was a multitude of fine details.

As David worked, he told me that he used to love to make car models and that his favorite part was painting details. "You know," he said, "I'd forgotten about that. It's been so long."

I knew from reading his medical chart that David had been married, but that his wife had died during childbirth. The baby, his daughter, had died too. That had been about five years before he came to treatment. In that time, he had resigned from his job as an insurance representative, withdrawn from his family, and lost his house and most of his friends. David's chart also indicated that the treatment team was concerned that he was talking to no one on the unit and avoided appointments with his psychotherapist. Although he had ample insurance resources, it was feared that if he did not begin to engage more actively, his coverage would be denied, and he would have to leave treatment.

As the painting neared completion, he expressed concern that the painting was "too dark."

"Well, David, I'm not so sure," I said. "In fact, I've been wondering if you shouldn't try to make it darker."

He replied: "I don't understand, Bruce. Why do you say that?"

"It seems to me that you are interested in everything in your life staying as gloomy as possible," I said. "I just thought that maybe you might want to darken some of these areas on your painting."

In an exasperated tone, David said: "But I just told you that I was thinking about trying to make it lighter. Now you say make it darker. That doesn't make any sense at all."

"David, I think that when we create things, we are making self-portraits," I explained. "If you add light to this forest, I think that you'll have to see what is there more clearly."

"So what's your point?" he asked.

"My point, David, is that if you start to see in the darkness of your woods, you'll also have to start to see in the gloom of your life," I said.

He sat back, thought for a moment, and said: "Bruce, when Susan and the baby died, I thought I never wanted to see another good thing ever again. It really has been like this woods: dark, frightening, and lonely. I don't know why, but I just got tired of talking about it with people, or they got tired of hearing about my misery, so I shut down. Somehow, and I don't understand it, doing this painting has made all that clear to me. People have said so many nice things about this place. It's made me want to see more. Will you teach me how to make moonlight? I want it to be on the tree limbs and grass."

I gave David a brief lesson in light and shadow. He did the rest.

The painting gave David an opportunity to express the grief and anguish that he had run out of words to express. With each motion of the brush and dip into midnight blue, he told his tale of loneliness and sorrow. The imaging of the story allowed him to move beyond its confines. The creative act allowed him to reclaim his right to author his own life. He no longer surrenders to the twist of fate that had ensnared him. His darkness has light, and his life goes on.

Curative Aspect Three: Art as Soul

The first time I remember hearing *art* and *soul* in the same sentence was in a conversation with a client in the late 1970s. She said, "My pictures are the windows to my soul." I don't think I fully understood her comment at the time; I thought she was merely being poetic. As is often the case, it took me a long time to appreciate the truth of her words (Figure 14).

The notion of art and soul being in some intimate relationship slept undisturbed within me for years after that conversation. It was reawak-

Figure 14. *Pictures are the Windows to my Soul*–Acrylic on canvas.

ened in the mid-80s by the works of McNiff and C. H. Moon. In *Depth Psychology of Art,* McNiff (1989) worked with the nomenclature of the art therapy profession and asserted that we should revisit our roots in a view of the arts as an unconscious religion. He also brought to the forefront the interrelationship of psyche and soul, suggesting that images are expressions of soul. C. H. Moon (1989) presented a paper at the national conference of the AATA, *Art as Prayer,* in which she attempted to "validate the unique gift of art as therapy because of its link to spirituality and prayer" (p. 126). That was, I believe, the first presentation at the national level that focused on an exploration of the common ground between the arts, therapy, and spirituality.

When therapeutic arts in a hospital or clinic setting are viewed from a perspective of soul, the work of art therapy is made sacred: Clients' images cannot be regarded as indicators of pathology, but rather as heartfelt portraits of selfhood. I believe that art comes from the depths of human experience, out of passion, conflict, and creative turmoil. Hillman (1989) describes soul as a perspective that transforms random events into meaningful experiences. This suggests that making art is a way of participating in soul. Art processes offer new perspectives, imaginative portraits of the artist and world. Paintings, drawings, sculptures, and other art forms make meanings visible by turning casual events into ensouled experiences. There is an artistic foundation to human existence that cannot be pinpointed as property of behavior, language, or physiology. The exceptional gift of art therapists to clients and clinical settings is the soul art-making process. This is work that only art therapists can do.

One's personal faith, be it Judaic, Christian, Buddhist, Muslim, or secular humanist, is often reflected in the art one creates. As an art therapist, I view the work I do as a sacred journey that my clients and I go on together. Our means of transportation is the doing of artistic work. Our primary form of communication is the sharing of images that emerge in artworks we create in the context of our relationship. The art products are the visual parables and prayers that mark the pilgrimage. In the sanctuary of the art therapy studio, soul is made in the midst of imaged confessions, thanksgivings, supplications, and praises. Being an art therapist is sacred, for the doing of art opens to us the mystery that is within our clients and ourselves. It is sacred to look through the soul windows of others. Making art is making soul (Figure 15).

Figure 15. *Making Art is Making Soul*–Acrylic on wood by Catherine Moon.

Linda Red and Black

Linda could speak, but she wouldn't. A victim of years of sexual and physical abuse, and emotional neglect, she seemed to have run out of words to say.

When she was referred to the expressive art therapy group, I wondered how it would be for her. While talking about one's artwork was not the group's primary focus, it was a component of the group process, and I was unsure how other group members would react to Linda's self-imposed silence. During the first session, as I explained the group structure, Linda made fleeting eye contact with me, but quickly averted her gaze. "Linda, this is a group where we use drawing as a way of getting in touch with, and sharing, feelings," I said. "You don't have to be Picasso or anybody like that. Whatever you do will be okay. The only thing I ask is that when someone else is speaking, we all pay attention. I believe that everybody in this group has a long history of people not taking their feelings seriously. In this group, we will always take your feelings seriously. Welcome to the group, I'm glad you are with us."

One of the other clients from Linda's living unit said, "I don't think that talking out of turn will be a problem for Linda." In a gentle and accepting way, other group members chuckled.

The beginning group ritual was to sit in a circle and briefly share feelings that each member was entering the group with that day. When it came Linda's turn, she held her arms tightly against her body and wrapped herself in a defensive cocoon. She rocked forward in her chair but said nothing. In a sense, Linda's body posture and motions expressed her feelings of vulnerability and anxiety. No words were necessary.

Addressing the group, I said. "Today, I want us to imagine a place that is safe. When the image comes, try to draw what you see."

We worked with vividly colored poster chalks on 3′ x 3′ sheets of brown craft paper taped to the wall. Without hesitation, Linda moved to a place at the wall and began to draw. She covered the paper quickly with solid red. She then used black to sketch a primitive rendering of what appeared to be a closet. The closet had a steeply slanted ceiling, a slatted door, and a pole with empty hangers dangling from it. In one corner, a figure was curled against the walls. When it came time to discuss her image, Linda shook her head and huddled in the same position as the figure in the drawing.

In many ways, that first session represented the entirety of Linda's involvement in the art therapy group. She eventually did say a few words, but never more than four or five in one session. Rather, she portrayed places, people, and happenings from her life in red and black images. The scenes were sometimes frightening, disturbing, or too mysterious for me to comprehend. But by creating images of these places and events, Linda ensouled them. She took time, and gave attention to people and places through her creative work. Often the people in her images were the ones who had treated her inhumanely, and the places were the scenes of the crimes against her. Yet, they were more than that, for Linda used her capacity to make to place herself in the position of the creator. By doing so, she ennobled her position, shifting from victim to heroine.

One remarkable day, Linda drew a fierce black panther about to pounce upon a small quivering child, as if to devour her. One of her peers in the group said: "Oh Linda, you poor thing. That beast looks like it is going to kill you."

Linda turned to her peer and replied, "I'm panther."

Her two-word sentence led group members into an intense discussion of their inner animal natures. When the group was wrapping up that day, I asked, "What are you leaving with today?"

Linda roared.

In the sanctuary of the studio, and the art therapy group room, soul is made as imaged confessions, thanksgivings, pleas, and praises are arted out. The making of images opens us to the mystery within each person, client, and therapist. It is a sacred thing to look through the soul windows of another.

Some people in helping professions would say that because Linda did not verbalize her feelings, my imaginings about her pictures and discussion of her work as an example of participating in soul were hogwash. A counselor colleague once told me that if the client doesn't talk about things, no therapy occurs. Some would argue that therapeutic progress in Linda's case was not measurable or scientifically verifiable, ergo non-existent.

To such colleagues, I would respectfully respond that I was there. I saw her transform from a silent, frightened shell of a person to a quietly strong young woman. I saw Linda get well. Making art is making soul. Linda was able to create meaning from the awful and senseless events of her past. She created an imaginative portrait of herself from a new perspective: a panther. With each new drawing, she anchored herself to the artistic foundation of life, thereby giving herself the strength and courage required to embrace the depth, passion, and conflict of her inner world. She did so almost exclusively through images. She had no need of words.

Curative Aspect Four: Art as Mastery

Art therapists should respect the work and mastery of art processes and materials. This reverence must be applied to the image, client, and efforts of the art therapist. It can be evidenced in the drive toward mastery of both client/artist and artist/therapist. The sense of personal adequacy that results from mastery of artistic techniques and media is linked to self-discipline and inevitably leads to positive self-regard. From positive self-regard comes a sacred passion for life shown through authentic, creative, and vital interactions between the individual and world. Such interactions are inherently connected to the artist's skillful use of media. But technical competence is hollow without emotional investment of the artist. Still, the success of any artwork depends equally upon its capacity to communicate ideas and feelings, and its demonstration of the artist's competent handling of materials.

As art therapists, we should not rely exclusively upon the therapeutic benefit of passing cathartic expressions of our clients. We must also embrace the authority of formal artistic procedures and techniques on the quality of expression. Careful attention must be given to the constant evolution of our clients' mastery of art processes. These are as important as art therapists' interpersonal relationship skills, communications skills, understandings of development, and psychotherapeutic techniques.

Mastery may be described as the ability to organize and transform raw materials and experiences. The significance of artworks in the therapeutic setting is found as clients transform powerful destructive inner forces into constructive, meaningful art objects. The process of making art involves organizing chaotic emotional material into a coherent, restructured product. The turbulent swirl of feelings, sensations, actions, and relationships are markers of mental and emotional distress. The arts offer clients hope for clarity and balance by alleviating distress through making art.

As clients' experience of mastery grows in relation to a specific artistic task, confidence and self-esteem increase. A healthy and gratifying reciprocity is established among the artist, task, and product that is intra-psychically contagious. As clients/artists experience success in the ability to handle media and solve artistic problems, the capacity to deal with other aspects of life is enhanced. We art therapists must take seriously the quality of clients' artwork and our own. At every opportunity, we should encourage clients not only to vent feelings, but also to do so in a skillful and artistically articulate manner.

I have worked with clients who initially used the art therapy studio as a dumping ground for feelings they wished they didn't feel. For instance, some clients would complete one or more art paintings in a single 90-minute session. Their paintings often resembled mud. In such circumstances, I have insisted that the client take a break from emotional regurgitation and learn the mechanics of mixing color. Other clients have benefited from instruction in one- and two-point perspective. The artistic building blocks of perspective and color mixing have helped clients structure and organize their expressions in ways that allow for personal attachment to both the expressive process and final product. This is not to say that I want clients to create pleasant or pretty pictures. On the contrary, most times the artworks born in the studio are painful and raw, but I do insist that clients attend to quality in the work itself.

My contention that attention to quality must be given is based on the belief that mastery is indicative of caring. If I allowed clients to simply slop paint onto a canvas with no regard for quality, I would be telling them that I have no investment in their art, and thus no real interest in them. Likewise, if I approach my own artistic efforts in the therapeutic studio with anything less than a focused care in relation to quality, I would be modeling inattention to self.

I do not expect my clients to become accomplished artists, but I do encourage them to care about quality in their lives. I ask them to do their best, and I look for ways to help them be better than they believe they are capable of being. Making art is working toward mastery.

A Bottle, a Cup, and a Box of Tissues

Ronnie's early work in the studio was suggestive of colorful vomit. His style of using materials and tools was also reminiscent of regurgitation. He poured huge amounts of paint directly onto unprimed Masonite panels. He refused to invest time to apply gesso, and he was, as he put it, "Not about to fart around building something (a stretcher frame for canvas) that ain't even going to show when I'm done."

Initially, my colleagues in the art therapy studio encouraged Ronnie's efforts. They viewed his work as cathartic and expressive. I, however, had a different reaction: I saw his handling of the paint as excessive and wasteful. His refusal to go through the proper procedural steps of building a canvas and applying gesso seemed resistive and defensive. He often left paint-filled brushes unwashed in the sink, and had I not found and cleaned them, they would have been ruined.

After some time had passed with no notable change in Ronnie's involvement in the studio, and no discernible reshaping of his interactive style, which was responsible for his being hospitalized, I suggested to my colleagues that we were spinning our wheels with Ronnie. One of my colleagues irritably exhorted me to take clinical responsibility for Ronnie. After some thoughtful discussion, I agreed to do so.

Session One

"Ronnie, I'm going to be working with you for awhile here in the studio," I said.

"I don't need any help," he replied.

"I'm not sure that I agree with you, Ron," I said. "But whether we agree or not, I have been assigned to work with you."

He went about the task of gathering paint containers and brushes without responding. I said: "You won't be needing that stuff today, Ron. You see, I've been thinking about you a lot, and I think you might have some good skills, but you don't seem to be able to use them very effectively."

He looked at me with a mixture of irritation and curiosity. "What the hell are you talkin' about?"

I replied: "I haven't kept an exact count, but I think you've done about seven or eight paintings since you've been here. None of them were very well thought out, and technically you've made a lot of mistakes."

He snapped, "Who gives a . . ."

I interrupted: "I do, Ronnie. It's sort of like if I took you to the piano in the campus center and told you to just play. You could bang on the keys, make a lot of noise, and you might even be able to convey some kind of feeling. But you would not be able to make music."

He stared at me wide-eyed and asked, "So you think my paintings are like noise?"

"Yes," I said. "They are okay for beginner's noise. But they are not the music that you could make. So let's put the paints away and start to work."

Reluctantly, he did as I asked. "Now what?" he said.

I gave him a 12″ x 18″ sheet of white drawing paper and #2 lead pencil. "We are going to start by learning to draw using perspective," I said. "First I need you to decide where the horizon line should be."

Ronnie's lessons in mastery had begun. He learned to do one-, two-, and three-point perspective drawings. He did them over and over. Then we shifted his attention to mastering the basic shapes: squares, rectangles, circles, ovals, triangles, cylinders, cones, and spheres. Next, he learned to shade, not with the side of the pencil, but with the point and a gentle touch. I often told him, "Use the six Ps: Prior Planning and Patience Provide for Positive Performance." He learned.

After the elemental steps of perspective, shape, and shading were understood, I placed a green bottle, plastic cup, and box of facial tissues on the table before him. "Draw these," I said. He began immediately and confidently to draw the shapes. The look on his face as he completed this drawing was a mixture of awe and pride. His peers in the studio were quick to praise his efforts, and the pleasure this brought Ronnie was obvious to everyone.

Ronnie made significant progress in terms of his mental health while hospitalized, not through cathartic expressive processes but by learning to struggle with quality in his work. In an artistic sense, he lived out the attention to quality that is described in Pirsig's (1974) *Zen and the Art of Motorcycle Maintenance.*

Art therapists must take the quality of our client's artwork seriously. We should not delude ourselves by thinking that expression is the only end of the arts in therapy. At every juncture, we can encourage clients not only to exorcise the emotions that haunt them, but also to develop artistic skills. Often clients initially seem to view the art therapy studio as a metaphoric garbage dump for feelings they long to discard. My insistence that attention be given to mastery and quality is anchored in the belief that *mastery* and *care* are synonymous. My investment in clients' lives and well-being is evident in my interest in their creations. I have no expectation that my clients become great artists, but I do expect them to learn to take care in their work, which in turn encourages them to care about quality in their own lives.

Curative Aspect Five: Art as Personal Metaphor

A metaphor is a manner of speaking in which one thing is described in terms of another; this sheds light on that which is being described and has the possibility of multiple interpretations. While the above description addresses the verbal dimensions of metaphor, it is insufficient for creative arts therapists. For our work, the idea that artworks, images, and actions can be metaphoric is more satisfactory. Artistic metaphors have both conscious and unconscious symbolic meanings for artists that articulate, express, define, and liberate their creator. This is an essential curative aspect of the art therapy discipline.

Metaphoric artworks contain an inherent quality of comparison in which one thing (the art object) is used to shed light on the character of the artist; the reverse is also true. Just as verbal metaphors hold the possibility of many divergent interpretations, so too do visual and action metaphors.

Art therapists are in an extraordinary position to see and respond to the metaphoric creations of our clients. We must honor the view of the poet Richter (1804), who posited that art may best be interpreted by a second artistic presentation. This suggests that the proper interpretive response to an artwork is not assignment of a fixed meaning or label but, rather, creation of another artwork. Art therapists should not enslave clients' artworks through verbal interpretations; rather, we should promote appreciation and a sense of awe, and dedicate ourselves to the notion that artworks can and should just be.

Everything artists create are partial self-portraits. I am not suggesting that this is all artworks are, but it is one important aspect of therapeutic and clinical interest to art therapists. To experience the depth and dramatic immediacy of art therapy, we need only to look at and be with our clients' images. We hardly need to talk at all.

To communicate with colleagues from other disciplines, art therapists must be able to verbally describe images and experiences to help colleagues grasp the potency and depth of art experiences that do not rely on words. Within the confines of the art therapy studio, art therapists should trust images and artworks to convey their own meanings.

Art therapists should value the communications presented in the artistic process and product even though artistic metaphors hold the potential for multiple interpretations. Making art is making personal metaphor.

Kerry and the Dog

When Kerry came to the hospital, she was a 21-year-old, overindulged, and spoiled college student living with her parents. She experienced severe panic attacks, particularly when her parents planned to be away from home. Kerry's father was a successful business executive who regularly traveled and often asked his wife to accompany him. These ventures were frequently disrupted by outrageous and self-defeating behaviors by Kerry. In the months prior to her hospitalization, Kerry's actions had become more dramatic and destructive. On one occasion, she drank alcohol to excess, took a handful of aspirin, and drove her late model sports car into a tree. She was lucky to be alive.

As Kerry participated in the art therapy group, I sometimes found myself irritated by her obnoxious and socially oblivious manner. To put it bluntly, she was a snob. She denied that her parents had anything to do with her difficulties, and she was often stubborn and immature.

It troubled me that I was having such a negative reaction to Kerry, so I discussed my feelings about her with my supervisor. He suggested that I try to focus more on the messages conveyed by her artworks and less on her overt behavior.

I began to listen to the stories she told as she described her drawings. During one session, it struck me that the reason her struggle with emancipation aroused such irritation in me was that it recalled feelings of anxiety and fear that I had lived through during my emancipation process. Though her wealthy, overly indulgent parents were different from mine, the feelings were not. How dare she make me remember?

Kerry often drew an image of a disheveled dog. Whenever she was asked about it, she would shrug her shoulders and say that it was just something she liked to draw. Rather than push for a cognitive explanation of this recurrent image, I decided to create an imaginal dialogue with it. I began the next session by telling this story:

Outside a certain town, at a certain time not too long ago, a man was traveling by car when he ran out of gas. As he walked through the countryside toward the next town, he came upon a dreadful sight. Beside a rundown old shack, there was a rundown old doghouse. In front of the doghouse lay an old mongrel licking an open wound on its side. One of the dog's eyes was swollen shut, and his hide looked as if it had been years since he'd been bathed.

The man was moved with pity, and he approached the animal. As he grew closer, he saw even more evidence of mistreatment. The traveler was appalled. He said, "Oh you poor thing."

Since this was a magical land, the dog raised his head and said, "Are you talking to me?"

"Yes," the man replied. "Yes, my God, how did you get to be such a mess?"

Without hesitating, the dog said: "It's my master. He has many stresses in his life. When he comes home from work, he beats me."

The man felt even more compassion and said: "Well, why do you stay here? Your tether is rotted. Surely you could run away."

The dog blinked his good eye and said, "But he always feeds me so well."

After my story, I asked the group to draw their responses. Kerry's drawing was full of rage at the dog's master. As the group members talked about their drawings, Kerry blurted out, "All I have to say is that the food must be pretty damned good!"

Another client in the group turned to Kerry and asked, "Well, how good is it, Kerry?" She fumed momentarily and then began a mixed laughing/crying session. She had discovered at least one of the meanings of her recurrent drawings of the disheveled dog.

At an unspoken level, Kerry's dog drawings had been trying to get the message to Kerry that it was time to grow up, even if growing up meant not always being as well-fed as she had been accustomed to. Kerry did not immediately change her life as a result of her metaphoric drawings and my story response to them, but she did cease to resist dealing with the role that her relationship with her parents played in her self-defeating behaviors.

By responding to her metaphor with a metaphor of my own, I helped Kerry see herself in the mirror of her drawings. I am not implying that this was all there was to Kerry or that there was only one meaning in her image of the dog. There was more to her than dependence, as there was more to the dog than hunger.

In this interchange, I did not make a fixed interpretation of her artwork, but rather engaged in an imaginative interpretive dialogue that allowed Kerry to participate with her metaphors. I believe that had I attempted to label or make a literal analysis of drawings, she would have withdrawn from the group and me before we could help. Any interpretive labeling on my part would have killed the image messenger and ultimately harmed the client/artist.

Curative Aspect Six: Art as Empowerment

In most instances, the persons who come to art therapists as outpatients, or who are treated in a residential facility, whether for psychiatric or physical reasons, come with a sense of disenfranchisement. They believe their personal power has been wounded. They often feel victimized by family, friends, or the world itself. It is essential that art therapists work with clients to restore their awareness and faith in their own power.

Empowerment is not a phenomenon that can be accomplished through verbalization alone. Experiences must foster the reclamation of power and the responsibilities that accompany it. Art therapists are in an ideal position to facilitate the process of empowerment in our clients by virtue of our own experiences with art-making. Art therapists are first initiated into the curative and transformative nature of artistic work through our own empowering engagements with media and processes. Art brings meaning to life by transforming conflict and ennobling painful struggle.

Struggle is essential to human nature. The collision of internal forces is often what brings about the creative actions of art. An important task for art therapists is to inspire in our clients a desire to use discomfort rather than be abused by it. The act of empowerment is a process of transformation from the position of victim to that of hero or heroine.

Human beings are a conglomerate of opposing forces, inconsistencies, and contradictions. We are in a state of continual change. Conflict and struggle are inevitable. There is a core tension within the self that is expressed through our polarities. Art does not lessen this tension, but rather often accentuates it by using the energy in empowering actions. Artists create meaning in their lives as they shape and color the distressing disharmony within them. Creating does not banish pain or discomfort, but rather it honors experiences that are difficult. Through the creative process of art-making, contradictions and conflicts are brought into focus that makes no sense. The empowering nature of art therapy does not seek to cure; instead, it accepts and ennobles the struggles of life. Art brings our fears, loneliness, and anguish close to us. It does not rid us of difficulties, but rather it enables us to live courageously in their presence.

The process of creating art is a metaphor for life because as artists work, they have the ultimate power to change the picture. They can add color, darken, or highlight. Artists can, if they choose, paint over the piece and start again. This is an allegory of life itself. Artwork and life can be changed if and when people decide to change. Many times, clients do not believe they have such power over the course of their lives, and art-making becomes an introduction into free will, and the power of choice and creation. Making art empowers.

To empower means to give official authority or legal power to, or enable. People seeking therapy often feel disempowered. Frequently, they view themselves as victims of those who have more power. Family members, friends, and the world are experienced as hostile and disenfranchising.

Sharon and the Sea

Sharon had heard about art therapy and my private practice from a friend. She told me during our first telephone contact that she felt "a little funny" about calling a therapist of any kind. When I asked what she meant, she explained that she wasn't sure her problems required professional help. "Maybe I'm just feeling sorry for myself," she said with a sigh. After several minutes of conversation, she said that she wanted to come into the office to meet me, but that she was making no commitment to "really be in therapy." I assured her that whatever she decided would be fine, and that I was willing to meet with her and give her time to make up her mind.

When Sharon arrived at my office, I was struck by my positive first impressions of her. While I would not describe myself as overly cautious in new relationships, I would say that I tend to take my time warming up to people. Sharon, though, had an instantly positive impact upon me. She appeared to be in her late 40s or early 50s. A tall woman of medium build, she carried herself in a comfortable but dignified manner. As she introduced herself to me, she established and held eye contact.

She quickly shared that she felt funny about seeking therapy for the difficulties of her life, including the recent death of her husband; unresolved feelings of anger toward her father who had been a distant and demanding figure; and her son's departure from home to college. There was sadness in her eyes, and I sensed that this was a new experience for her. She had always been surrounded by people who could support her through struggles; now, she found herself facing profound losses with no shoulder to cry on.

Despite having really good reasons for seeking therapy, Sharon said, "I'm still not exactly sure why I am here, Mr. Moon."

I replied: "I don't know exactly why you've come to me either, Sharon. You did say on the phone that a friend had told you about me. Is that right?"

"Yes," she said.

"Let's start there," I said. "What did your friend tell you?"

"She said that you helped her daughter a few years ago when she was a teen-ager," she said.

"Something about what she said must have sounded appealing," I replied.

"I think it was that she told me that you and her daughter painted pictures together," she said.

"You'd like to learn to paint?" I asked.

"Yes, I've always wanted to, but I never took the time," she said.

"You have time now?" I asked.

She sighed and said, "Yes, too much time." Her eyes brimmed with tears, and we sat in silence for a few moments. She continued: "My husband Tom and I were planning to go to Hilton Head Island this spring. We were there once, a long time ago, and we always said we'd get back there. But we were so busy."

Sensing the poignancy and richness of this discovery, I said, "We could paint the sea if you decide to get into therapy."

"I wouldn't know where to begin," she said.

I smiled, "I know how to start, but you would have to help me."

"How could I help you?" she asked.

"You'd have to describe the place that you want to paint in great detail," I said.

Sharon said, "Oh, I could do that, all right."

This was how Sharon entered into art therapy: She was struggling with feelings of loss and loneliness, but still interested in life. She did not seem overtly bitter or angry about her situation, just overwhelmed. By the end of that first interview, I was sure that I wanted to help Sharon, and confident that engaging in art processes would benefit her. She agreed, and we decided to meet on a weekly basis for one hour.

She began to tell me stories about the sea. She painted and shared night walks on the beach, wind storms, and skinny dipping on a lonely stretch of shoreline south of Kitty Hawk, North Carolina.

I responded by demonstrating wash and overlay techniques, suggesting that a touch more white be added to the ultramarine, and helping her with light glints on her waves.

Sharon completed three paintings while in therapy. The first portrayed her and Tom huddled against the wind as a stormy sea crashed against a rocky shoreline. The second depicted them sitting side by side gazing at a sunset over calm water. In the third painting, Sharon stood facing the horizon alone. The sea was rough but not overwhelming, and the sky was clear.

Through the making of these three paintings, Sharon ennobled her struggle with letting go of her husband and getting on with her life. She transformed her pain into images. This did not make the pain go away, but it helped her accept it. Sharon stopped being controlled by her feelings of loneliness and abandonment, and was able to use those feelings as the source of her creative work. This enabled her to live courageously in the presence of her loss. The paintings provided a metaverbal chronicle of her therapeutic work. She moved from the position of the clinging person caught in a storm to that of a loving wife celebrating memories with her husband. Finally, the third painting portrayed a woman standing alone in daylight. The sea was not calm or overpowering. The natural turmoil of this phase of Sharon's life was dramatically represented. As she discovered the artistic power of painting over, reworking, and changing direction with her paintings, Sharon embraced her power over her own existence.

Curative Aspect Seven: Art as Work

The sum of an artist's production is described as work. The body of this work is the aggregate of the artist's capacity to put forth effort, toil, and exhibit patience as the labor unfolds. The body of work is a concrete measure of the artist's tolerance of the internal dynamism that both seethes and soothes.

The viewing audience often only sees the finished work, not the work that was required prior to exhibition. The labor of artists is neither easy nor comfortable. There are many sore muscles, strained eyes, blistered hands, and hearts that conspire and collaborate to create. Making art is work.

In art therapy, respect for the artwork of both the client and therapist is necessary. The art therapist cannot depend exclusively upon the impermanent cathartic efforts of the client. Consideration must also be given to the weight of rigorous artistic techniques on the quality of the expression. Such labors demand passionate discipline on the part of the art therapist. The client's willingness to take the therapeutic journey is directly influenced by the art therapist's enthusiasm and work ethic. The art therapist's passionate discipline can be seen in the art therapist's own artwork. As we paint, draw, or sculpt, we rediscover the meaning of our work as art therapists. It is in our own studio that we experience struggle and confusion, the artistic frustrations that are integral to our work as therapists.

Just as making art is neither easy nor comfortable, being in therapy for clients is neither effortless nor relaxed. The labors of artists and clients are marked by sore muscles, and blistered hands and hearts. Art and therapy are hard work. "To be sure, all of this is done in order to create something for which reason we can call it work and not rage" (Menninger, 1942, p. 134).

Clients come to art therapy to involve themselves in the creative work of transforming destructive energy into constructive ends. They come to work out potent intra- and interpersonal conflicts. This is hard work.

The sense of mastery derived from creative work is integrally connected to the development of self-discipline, which is ultimately connected to pleasure. From artistic work grows a sacred passion for life as it is. This sacred passion is marked by authentic, creative, and vital involvement with materials, the self, and others. Engaging in art tasks establishes a therapeutic milieu in which destructive forces are transformed into meaningful objects. Making art is a process of organizing millions of imaginal possibilities that swirl in a chaotic mass of potential. Art therapy is a process of organizing the turbulent and chaotic inner feelings, sensations, conflicts, and behaviors that are the signposts of emotional distress. Again, this is hard work.

Allen, I See What You Have Made

Allen was in his late 30s when I first met him. He came to the hospital after a series of bizarre acts that resulted in his being arrested on two occasions. The police had threatened him with detention after several other incidents of strange behaviors. He was a tall and gangly man with deep-set eyes encased by dark circles. He dressed sloppy and exhibited poor personal hygiene habits: His teeth were yellow, as were the tips of his fingers on his left hand, from chain-smoking unfiltered cigarettes. He seldomly spoke to members of the treatment staff or his peers.

He was diagnosed with chronic schizophrenic disorder with paranoid features. The early impression of the psychiatry resident assigned to be Allen's medical manager was that his hospital stay would be brief with the primary goal being to stabilize him on psychotropic medications and return him to his marginal level of functioning at home. The psychiatrist supervising the young resident was confident that Allen would derive little benefit from anything other than psychopharmacology. The psychiatrist echoed his student's view that Allen's condition was not hopeful, and that perhaps the best the treatment team could do was contain his disturbing acting-out behaviors "until the medicine kicked in."

Despite this limited treatment plan and dismal prognosis, the resident did not object to Allen being placed in a full regimen of therapeutic activities that included studio art, greenhouse, and leisure sports. The head nurse expressed concern that, "He won't really do what you want him to, and you people will have to watch him like a hawk."

Early in his involvement in the art therapy studio, Allen was asked to do a variety of creative assessment activities that included painting, drawing, and collage-making. Although he was cooperative and seemed to make a genuine effort, his artistic products were crude and poorly executed. Allen remained non-communicative.

One morning, the art therapy staff was busy due to an influx of new clients who needed to be oriented to the studio and the activities. Allen stood quietly by the sink, seeming to be in his own world. No one paid attention to him until one of my colleagues noticed that Allen had bent a coffee can serving as a water container. My peer confronted him about abusing materials. I sensed that Allen's bending the can was neither malicious nor random. He was attempting to shape the brightly colored metal. I intervened and asked Allen to follow me to the tool cabinet, where I gave him a pair of metal shears and needle-nosed pliers. Without looking at me he said, "Thank you."

He then proceeded to work, shaping, cutting, and bending the coffee can into the form of a whimsical bird. As the session neared its end, he approached me and asked, "Thread?"

"Sure, Allen, what color would you like?" I asked.

"Yellow," he said.

He attached a three-foot piece of thread to the body of the bird, then hung it from a nail above a doorway. Whenever someone passed under it, the wind of the passer-by gently nudged the bird. It appeared to float in the air. Allen smiled.

Clearly, initial attempts to involve Allen in two-dimensional creative acts missed the mark, but three-dimensional work engaged him. Working from this hypothesis, I introduced him to a form of stone sculpture.

In that setting, it was not possible to work with traditional stone sculpture materials. Stone sculpture processes are too time-consuming and cost-prohibitive. We did, however, find an acceptable alternative solution. We made our own stone by blending concrete mix and vermiculite. By altering the amount of vermiculite added to the mixture, we manipulated the hardness and resistance of the material such that the more vermiculite, the softer the block.

The average block of stone we made was two cubic feet. Allen fell in love with that material, and the tools used to chip, cut, and shape it. He hammered and chiseled, and filed and sanded, piece after piece. As the chips fell, graceful shapes emerged. Abstract masses that were both energetic and elegant hinted at animal forms. Allen's hammer and chisel breathed life into the inanimate gray concrete.

This was not an easy enterprise. As his confidence and skill level grew, he asked for harder stone blocks to work with for finer, more detailed pieces. It was hard work. His hands blistered, and he sweated. His muscles strained as he pounded, smoothed, and gouged the stone.

Allen did not cease to struggle with the symptoms of schizophrenia as a result of his involvement with the hammer, chisel, stone, and me. But he did create several intriguing artworks from hunks of gray concrete and vermiculite. Meanwhile, we established a camaraderie that was different from the isolated and detached stance he had maintained before he came to the hospital. Did his engagement with coffee cans and stone take away his paranoid ideation? No. Did his consistent participation in creative arts sessions, once daily, five days a week, improve his personal hygiene? Not really. Then what was the point of his being in art therapy at all?

In the time he spent in the hospital, Allen made at least a dozen sculptures. He let people watch him as he worked. Sometimes he would respond when they asked a question. Sometimes his face lit up as he watched another human being touch the smooth edge of one of his works. I believe that Allen made contact with the world in a way that he had never done before. There may be no psychological measuring sticks to quantify the qualitative difference that creating art made in Allen's life. Measurable or not, there was a difference that could be felt more than seen. When I last heard from him, he wrote a short letter indicating that he had switched to woodcarving. He wrote, "It's a lot easier to clean up the mess."

I do not know if Allen became any more "functional" in the practical sense of the word, but I have faith that Allen's inner world and the larger community have been enriched by his artistic work.

Curative Aspect Eight: Art as Play

Much of the work of art therapists involves being with clients' images that are raw, painful, and horrific. These images come from the depths of persons struggling with problematic issues. Thank goodness making art is fun! For all of the demons and shadows, there are angels, jesters, and bright places lurking within clients, waiting their turn on the imaginal stage. Art therapists must have faith that such images are as willing to share their joys as are inner monsters dispensing terrors. This is why the faces of children light up as their crayon scribbles are taped to the refrigerator door. This is part of the fun.

The adult clients/artists I have treated are typically hyperaware of the pain and discomfort that emerge in their artworks, but the fun and play involved in making art enables clients/artists to face the disturbing aspects of their creative endeavors. Artful play offers clients a dynamic source of energy, and there is often a whimsical quality to art that allows emotion and mystery into the realm of clients' daily lives.

The infusion of play and imagination brightens the routine and familiar. An inherent curative aspect of art is that it brings pleasure, allowing clients to contend with, and take part in, life. Play encourages people to explore freedom and limits through the use of imagination and activity. Making art is a form of play (Figures 16 & 17).

Figure 16. *Playing*–Tempera on paper.

Figure 17. *Making Play*–Marker on paper.

Artistic play makes a dynamic source of energy available to us. Art brings pleasure and promotes a sensual relationship with the environment. The sculptor feels the impact of chisel against stone. The dancer feels the weight of body on feet. The ceramicist feels the slippery ooze of wet clay spinning on the potter's wheel. The painter smells linseed oil and senses the roughness of the canvas as the brush pushes pigment across the surface. Art processes demand that artists touch the world.

There is an imaginal and mysterious quality to art that allows emotions, fantasies, and wishes into our daily lives. The arts evoke and intensify feelings, providing a safe structure for expression that is often fun.

Sandy's Dance

Sandy was admitted to the hospital the day before she was referred to the art therapy group. When she entered the group room, she moved slowly as if she were carrying a heavy weight. I introduced her to other group members and explained, "This is a group in which we use drawing as a way of getting in touch with and sharing feelings." I asked her if she had ever tried to draw her feelings.

Sandy replied, "No, I haven't drawn anything since I left elementary school."

"Well, that's good, this'll really be something new and different for you," I replied.

Sandy asked: "Why did they want me to be here? It sounds a little childish to me."

"I suppose some people might think that it is silly," I said. "But, I think it's a good thing to express your feelings, and using art can be a fun way to do so."

Sandy did not seem convinced. "So, what are we supposed to do?" she asked.

I replied: "In a moment, I'll give the group a theme to work from, and then we'll draw for awhile. When we're done, we'll spend some time talking about the pictures. At the end of the session, we'll take the drawings off the wall, and you can either take yours with you or throw it away."

Sandy grimaced and asked, "What's the point of doing it if you are just going to throw it away?"

"You can keep your drawings if you want to, Sandy, but that's not the point," I said.

Another group member said, "You'll get used to it. It is a little embarrassing at first, but Bruce always says 'trust the process,' and it can really feel good sometimes."

Addressing the group, I said, "Today, as a way of getting warmed up, I'd like you to close your eyes and imagine yourself dancing." After a couple of minutes, I said, "Now I want you to get a piece of chalk in both hands, and again with your eyes closed, move against your paper. Let your hands make the dance."

There were some groans, but eventually everyone was doing what I'd asked them to do. As the chalk/dance noises came to an end, I told members of the group to open their eyes and look at the dance drawings on the wall.

Sandy's dance was drawn in sky blue and white. The image had a light, delicate, and airy feel. I commented that it reminded me of a ballet.

Sandy said: "When I was a little girl, I used to imagine that someday I would be a famous dancer. My brother used to make platform stages for me out of cardboard, and I would dance and dance."

I responded, "Your drawing seems light and fanciful."

Sandy said: "There was a song . . . I think Judy Collins sang it. It was about a girl whose father always promised her someday they would live in France, and she could learn to dance. I loved that song." Tears appeared in her eyes.

"Yes," I said. "I know the song (Collins, 1972). It is beautiful like your drawing."

"I haven't thought of that game with my brother in 20 years," she said.

"Is it a good memory?" I asked. .

Sandy said, "It is good, but I feel sad thinking about it."

"What is it that stirs the sadness?" I asked.

She looked down at the floor and said: "It's been so long since I felt that way: free and able to dance. I can't even remember the last time I felt good about anything."

"Your drawing is very nice, Sandy," I said.

Sandy asked, "May I keep it?"

"Of course," I said. "It is yours."

There is tremendous therapeutic value inherent in the process of making art. There are fleeting qualities of perception, elusive bits of light and shadow, and sound and physical sensations captured as the client/artist moves across the page with chalk in hand.

Some of the words associated with play are to: move swiftly, touch lightly, flutter and vibrate, and contend with and take part. To move freely, especially within prescribed limits, inspires work and action. As Sandy's hospitalization continued, it was fascinating to watch her regain her life force. In the art therapy group room and fine arts studio, Sandy rediscovered her capacity to play. Artistic play reacquainted her with her own dynamic internal energy, and this allowed her to deal with the past as she experimented with her imagination in the present.

Curative Aspect Nine: Art as Relationship

Throughout the history of humanity, relationships among individuals have been important. This is evident in the development of one person, as well as in the evolution of a group, nation, or culture.

Commenting on human beings serving their own interests and conforming to the interests of the group to which they belong, Goldschmidt (as cited in Hamburg, 1963) suggests that every person longs for responses from the human environment. This longing may be expressed as a desire for connection, acknowledgment, acceptance, support, positive regard, or mastery.

In relation to art, perhaps the longing for human response partially explains why prehistoric humans stained the walls of caves, and why Rouault painted and Rodin sculpted. The act of making is an invitation to relate. By making, the artist takes images from within and gives them visible form in the world. In a sense, art-making is an act of acknowledgment of one other beyond the boundaries of self. The other is the beholder, the audience.

Few things are more painful to the psyche than loneliness. Nearly every major trend in psychotherapy, with the exception of psychopharmacology, is anchored in theories involving interpersonal relationships.

Yalom (2005) states:

The theory of interpersonal relationships is presently so much an integral part of the fabric of psychiatric thought that it needs no underscoring. People need people—for initial and continued survival, for socialization, for the pursuit of satisfaction. No one—neither the dying, nor the outcast, nor the mighty—transcends the need for human contact. (p. 24)

Personal meaning can be found only in the context of relationships. The self must be transcended for meaning and purpose to be present. Artists' works are best acknowledged in the domain of relationships. Art is inspired in the territory of interpersonal connection that is shared with human experience. The community must respond to the artist's work for the art process to be complete. It doesn't matters if the audience responds with praise or critique; what is important is that the community responds.

Through artwork, the artist offers a view, a unique response to the world. Although passive, the community receives the imaginal offspring of the artist's struggle. It is only in the context of relationship to the community that artists establish their particular identity. The other comprehends the uniqueness of the artist. The artist creates, the community responds, the artist makes again, the community attends, and so on. Art-making is relating.

Art-making is transcendent. Usually artists are interested in the reaction their work inspires in others. This interest is essentially motivated by desire for contact with others. A central curative aspect of art therapy is the capacity to promote the development of relationships. Although many artists profess that they are private beings and must be left alone to work, most still aim their creative work toward other people. Making art is thus concerned with community and deepening relationships.

The communities formed in art therapy groups I've led have vested me with a level of authority to work with the burdens clients bring. Clients cast their images upon the walls of the studio. Through rituals of creation, we engage in a process of acknowledgment of the way our lives are. The intent of arting out the painful pieces of self is to empower clients to grasp the meaning of their images. This is done in the company of others.

Michelle's Hands

The drawing seemed innocuous enough. Michelle had used black and white chalk on brown paper to depict two hands clutching a metal bar.

The group session, consisting of six emotionally disturbed adolescent girls, had been wild. One girl had come to session directly from the special care room (seclusion), where she'd spent the previous night in restraints due to suicidal ideation. Another girl was all wound up in anticipation of her first family therapy session. She'd been on "therapeutic separation" for three weeks. The other four members were, in varying degrees, angry, depressed, and resistive. It was one of those days when I felt I'd earned my salary just by containing the intense affect of the group.

Michelle's low-key drawing had not grabbed much attention. When it came her turn to share, she said quietly: "When I drew this, I wasn't sure I'd say anything about it to you. This is hard for me to look at."

I responded, "You don't have to say anything, Michelle."

"I know," she replied. "I'm not deaf, Bruce. I've heard you say that crap about a thousand times."

Calmly I said: "I just want you to know that I think it's most important that you do the art. Talking is okay, but it's not the main thing in this group."

"I know, now will you let me do this?" she asked. "This is a picture of my hands. They are holding on to the railing of the bed I used to sleep in when I was a little girl." She began to cry, and the room became quiet. "I used to hold onto the rail so tightly. I was so afraid." There were more tears. One of her peers moved her chair closer to Michelle's.

I got a box of tissues from the counter and laid it beside Michelle's chair.

"My dad used to get drunk and come into my room," she said. "I had to hold onto the rail, or else I was afraid I'd hit him or hurt him. He'd, you know . . . I loved him. Oh God, it makes me want to puke."

"You've been through a lot, Michelle," I said.

Addressing the whole group, I said: "You know, there are days in this group that I am awed by what happens here. What an honor it is for me to be with you all sometimes."

Michelle said, "This hurts so fucking bad."

I replied: "Michelle, I believe that things we draw are sort of like self-portraits. I also believe that you can change the picture if that's what you want to do."

She looked at me skeptically and asked, "What are you talking about?"

"You can change the image, Michelle," I said. "You aren't that little girl anymore. You can let go of the rail, you can draw fists, lock your bedroom door, or anything else you want."

"No, I want to keep this one the way it is," she said. "But I think I'll draw some more pictures like this."

Beth, another girl in the group, said, "Well, if I were you, I'd tear that damned thing off the wall."

"No, I just want to roll it up and keep it," she said. She stood and ceremoniously rolled the paper into a tight cylinder.

In sessions that followed, many scenes of Michelle's hands were drawn. She portrayed her hands gradually letting go of the bed rail. She gave them color, balled them into fists, and pounded them against images of her father. In a later work, she opened her hands, as if in a gesture of offering. With the support of her peers in the group, she moved from images of tight constriction, to rage, to consolation.

If, as I have suggested, art-making is soul-making, then we art therapists are shepherds of souls. We guide our clients as best we can toward experiences that nourish them. We watch out for danger, retrieve those who are lost, and help sustain the wounded. We do not send them out alone. By making art together, we accompany our clients and form relationships with them.

Curative Aspect 10: Art as Structure and Chaos

Clients often tell me that the most difficult stage of their art process is the beginning. As they stare at an empty canvas, they are overwhelmed by possibilities. There are so many options when the canvas is untouched. These potentials are endless and, thus, chaotic.

Every decision that the artist makes, beginning with deciding the size and shape of the canvas, limits options and brings order to the chaos of possibilities. When artists select oils, they close the door on acrylics, watercolors, and tempera. Through a myriad of decisions, the artist brings form to the chaos of inestimable possibilities. Decisions the artist makes relative to size, shape, form, and media are parallel to the internal process of filtering imaginal possibilities. How this thematic fermentation happens is a mystery.

In *Existential Art Therapy: The Canvas Mirror* (B. L. Moon, 1990, 1995), I use the metaphor of a boiling pot of seawater to conceptualize the process of thematic fermentation. As the water boils and turns to steam, it leaves a residue of salt. The salt was always there, but it took boiling to make it visible. Within the psyche of the artist, a similar process occurs as the artist's feelings, images, themes, conflicts, and powerful forces simmer, eventually showing the artist's "salt" in the form of a completed artwork.

Making art is always a process of structuring chaos. Whatever needs to be expressed will be expressed. Creating art is the process of constantly moving back and forth between order and disorder, spontaneity and composition, and chaos and structure. As the artist stands before an untouched drawing pad or sits before the uncentered clay spinning on the potter's wheel, the possibilities are infinite. All decisions the artist makes brings order and limits to the chaotic potential of the work not started. In the world of the artist, chaos demands process, which leads to structure and yields products. In the world of the suffering art therapy client, chaos demands process, which leads to structure and yields engagement in life.

Richard's Universe

At the psychiatric hospital, it was customary for a representative of the adjunctive therapy department to meet with newly admitted clients to design a regimen of therapeutic activities. During Richard's initial interview with the adjunctive therapist, he fell asleep. He was nine years old, and had Attention Deficit Hyperactive Disorder, Major Depression, and Adjustment Reaction. His biological parents had abandoned Richard when he was two months old. Since then, he'd been in a host of foster care and residential care settings. He had also been adopted at age six, and given back when he was eight.

He told the adjunctive therapist that he had no hobbies, interests, or curiosity about the activity therapy program at the hospital. The therapist had limited information to go on in terms of designing a therapeutic activity schedule for Richard. The next day, when she arrived at the unit, Richard was in seclusion. Two days later, she again approached him about his therapeutic activity schedule. This time, Richard was distracted and suspicious. His attention span was short.

The adjunctive therapist decided to schedule Richard into a horticulture activity group, physical education/recreation, and communication skills group. Within the first few hours of his involvement in these activities, Richard was sent back to the unit from each area due to his swearing, spitting, and kicking. In the physical education group, his explosive behavior frequently got him involved in altercations with his peers and the recreation therapists. In the greenhouse, he isolated and did things "my way or not at all." In the communication skills activity, he manifested a variety of bizarre behaviors that set him apart from his peers and reinforced his negative self-view.

I was asked to consult with the adjunctive therapist about Richard and suggest ways the milieu could become more supportive and beneficial to him. As I read his medical chart, social history, and results of his psychological testing, I suspected that there was a consistent element of chaos in Richard's life. He'd attended many schools despite only being in the third grade. He'd lived in a number of homes and residential treatment facilities. When I tried to imagine how the world must have looked to Richard, words like chaotic, unsure, threatening, and disappointing came to mind.

I suggested to the adjunctive therapist that the psychiatric team consider limiting Richard's activities and relationships. I sensed that Richard needed the stability of a consistent daily schedule and predictable relationships. The treatment team agreed, and Richard was withdrawn from his activities. A small cadre of nurses and attendants were designated his primary caregivers. I was asked to provide individual art therapy sessions on a daily basis.

In the early stages of individual art therapy, Richard was literally all over the room. He opened drawers and cupboards, filled water containers, splashed in the sink, stuck his fingers in paint, knocked the trash can over, pulled paper towels from the dispenser, and flicked the lights on and off. He reminded me of a human version of the Tasmanian devil cartoon character.

In response to his whirling dervish behavior, I instituted a plan to begin therapy by setting clear limits. I limited our sessions to 15 minutes and insisted that he ask me before touching things in the studio. If he did not comply with this rule, I would give him one warning; if he continued to break the rule, I would return him to the unit. Several sessions only lasted five or 10 minutes. But gradually, as Richard became assured that no matter how badly he behaved on one day, I would keep our appointment the next day, he settled into a routine.

He would often begin sessions by growling: "I hate this darn place. What are we gonna do today?"

My response was consistent, "Richard, we're going to make something."

"What are we gonna make?" he'd grumble.

"What would you like to make, Richard?" I'd reply.

This became our ritual of initiation. From this simple beginning, Richard's creations grew. Several sessions into our therapy relationship, Richard asked if he could make something out of cardboard. I told him that the only cardboard in the studio was from old supply boxes.

He said, "That's just the kind I want."

When I brought two old boxes from the storeroom, he dove into them with scissors. Without a plan, he cut shapes, pasted, and glued, creating his rendition of "Star Trek's" *U.S.S. Enterprise.* During that session, he worked non-stop for 30 minutes.

The *Enterprise* was the first of a galaxy of cardboard creations. He made a Klingon warship, a Romulan vessel, Federation freighters, planets, suns, and moons.

I have often wondered if his medium of choice, cardboard, preferably of the discarded variety, in some way represented his sense of self: if he felt he had been thrown away by the adult world. I did not ask Richard about this. I saw no point in putting this interpretation into words because I could think of no way the words would help him.

As Richard worked for longer periods of time in the art therapy studio, he got into fewer arguments at school and on the living unit. I believe that his creation of a cardboard galaxy symbolically helped him bring structure to the chaos of his own childhood universe. As he gave form to the chaotic discarded cardboard, he brought structure to his own disorder. Feelings, conflicts, and powerful forces were given form through the psychic salt of Richard's artworks.

Curative Aspect 11: Art as Hope

Hope is an essential curative aspect of all forms of psychotherapy. Art therapists must have hope for their clients, and clients need hope for themselves. If there is no hope, there will be no therapeutic progress. It should be expected that a client's hope is endangered. The art therapist's hope, then, must be solid and unshakeable. Hope requires faith. Clients need to have faith in the art therapist, and art therapists must have faith in the art process, themselves, and the essential goodness and value of people. Making art is a symbolic expression of hope. In an unspoken manner, engaging in creative activity is a generative act, a way of giving to the next generation. To give in this way, one must believe that the next generation is worthy of the gift.

I have seen this principle repeatedly enacted in art therapy studios in residential facilities. Clients who have been in therapy awhile subtly welcome and initiate newcomers. The veteran client demonstrates to newly admitted clients that the treatment experience can be survived, and in fact, can be good. This message is conveyed verbally, behaviorally, and symbolically. Clients often donate artworks to the studios and facilities in which I have worked. These works are hung on the walls whenever possible. They stimulate the environment and, whether or not the new client knew the former client, share a powerful message: "Have faith and hope."

Critical in this hoping is the art therapist's conviction that what art therapists do is healthy and curative. Belief in the healthiness of art therapy is contagious. Likewise, any doubts that art therapists harbor about their contribution to the therapy process can negatively infect the air of the studio. Such messages, whether positive or negative, are not a matter of verbalization. They are subtle and covert. This is why art therapists should remain active artists. Faith in the art-making process is nurtured in the studio. Creating art is a declaration of faith and hope.

Judy and her Wall

Judy entered the studio quietly. She was 37 years old, but looked closer to 50. Her eyes were gray and dull. I knew from preliminary reports that she had been a gang member since late adolescence. She'd used marijuana daily, been an alcoholic, and occasionally snorted cocaine. She had a sunken yet hard appearance.

Judy admitted herself to the hospital. She showed up late one evening at the entrance to emergency services where she told the clinician that she would either be admitted to the hospital that night or dead the next morning.

As she came into the studio, her eyes were downcast, her hair was unkempt, and her clothes smelled of stale cigarettes. As I gave her a tour of the building, she stopped in front of a painting hung in the northeast comer. The image was an abstract portrait of an unborn infant and mother. The mother stood with her back arched as a swirl of dark colors surrounded her.

"Did you do that?" Judy asked.

"No, that painting was done by one of our adolescent clients last winter," I said.

Judy looked at me suspiciously and said, "I suppose you wouldn't let him take it home!" There was an edge of defiant hostility to her voice.

"Oh no," I replied. "He could have taken it with him, but he decided to leave it hanging here in the studio."

"Why would he do that?" she asked.

"Well, Judy, you'd really have to ask him to know for sure, but I think it was because he had a good experience in the hospital," I said. "He wanted to give something to the studio."

She grimaced and said: "That's a laugh. Who the hell has a good experience here?"

Overhearing this, Horace, a retired man who'd been coming to the art therapy studio about three weeks, said, "I have."

Judy turned toward Horace. "Who asked you?" she sneered.

Horace looked at his sculpture uncomfortably and said: "Nobody asked. But I heard what you said to Bruce. Really, lady, how do you expect him to answer your question? If he tells you that people sometimes end up liking it here, or that people get better here, you'll say that he's feeding you a line of B.S. There's no way for him to win. I've been here a couple of weeks, and I've seen this same thing happen several times. New people come in feeling like death-warmed-over, and Bruce tells them about how making art will help them. They look at him like he's nuts."

"Sounds loony tunes to me," Judy said.

Horace went back to his work and said, "You'll get out of this place what you put into it, lady."

Judy yawned. "I'm so bored," she said.

I said: "You know, Judy, boredom comes from an absence of quality relationships. I think Horace is right: You'll get what you give in the hospital. Let's get to work."

It is essential that we art therapists have a firm conviction that what we do is healthy and curative. If we have faith and trust in the power of the creative process, our faith will be infectious. Art therapists must remain active artistically, for it is in the doing of art for ourselves that faith is nurtured. It is in the studio that hope is kindled. Let's get to work.

Curative Aspect 12: Art as Benevolence

In the art therapy studio, clients often find their needs met as they give to others. These same clients, in early stages of therapy, may feel empty and barren, as if they have nothing of merit to offer another human being. Clients offer tremendous support and help to each other in the studio. They encourage one another, critique one another, share artistic techniques, make suggestions, and listen to one another. Outcome studies suggest that the relationships among clients formed in the context of the treatment situation have at least as much to do with the eventual success or failure of the therapy as do the professional therapists (Huestis & Ryland, 1990).

The making of art is an activity of self-transcendence. Clients in a psychiatric hospital are frequently morosely self-indulgent. Such self-absorption takes many forms, including hopelessness, excessive introspection, and unrelenting self-analysis. Yet it is clear, as Frankl (1969) discusses, that meaning can be found only in the context of relationship and transcending the self. Art-making absorbs the client in something outside the self. In the studio, this transcendent absorption is a public act. Clients respond to the artwork of other clients. There is a contagious benevolence that pervades the air of the art therapy studio. Making art is benevolent.

Frances and her Boxes

Frances had been in the art therapy group for three sessions. She was a middle-aged editor of textbooks. She was a precise, but controlling and cold woman. The artworks she created in the group were rigid and lifeless.

Addressing members of the group, I said: "Today I want us to begin by drawing five circles on your paper. Put your name at the top the page. Then, I'd like us to move around the room to others' papers and draw a symbol of your impressions of that person in one of their circles."

Frances said: "Oh, I don't think I could do that. I really don't know any of these people that well."

One of her peers replied: "Lighten up, Frances. You know us as well as we know you."

I said: "Give it your best effort, Frances. I'm sure that everybody is interested in how you see them."

Frances replied: "I'll just do the same thing on everyone's page then. Will that make you happy?" She glared at me.

I did not respond to Frances's angry baiting. Group members moved around the room attending to their images of one another. A discussion period followed the drawing portion of the session. When it came time to discuss the images drawn on Frances's page, the atmosphere of the group thickened. An air of tension filled the small room.

Tony said: "Frances, I tried to draw a brick wall. You seem so hard on yourself to me. You never bend, 'least I ain't seen it."

Frances reacted, "*Ain't* is not proper grammar, Tony."

Patricia asked, "Didn't you hear what Tony said, Frances?"

Frances replied, "I heard him quite distinctly."

Referring to her drawing, Patricia said: "I drew the boxes. They are all the same color and size. They are all in order, but it looks to me like something's missing, Frances."

Frances interrupted, "Well, I . . ."

Jim cut her off: "I drew your circle as gray. I wish I knew more about Frances, but I just couldn't think of anything colorful to draw about you."

Tears welled in Frances's eyes, but she tried to fight them.

I said: "It's all right, Frances. Let them come. Nobody here wants to hurt you, just let them come."

Frances's dam burst, and years of tears poured from her. Patricia picked up the tissue box and placed it beside her chair. She leaned over and gave her a hug.

In the art therapy studio and group room, clients meet their needs by giving to others. Sometimes the gifts are painful ones, and sometimes gentle and supportive. They often encourage one another and sometimes criticize. They share artistic and life strategies. They make suggestions and listen to each other. Benevolence is the disposition to do good. It is seen in acts of kindness. Making art can be a benevolent and generous act, for it is a gift to others, and offering to life itself.

Chapter 11

PATHOS OR PATHOLOGY

In my early professional life, I occasionally heard colleagues from other disciplines express fears about the role of artistic expression in therapy settings. One psychiatrist was concerned that art therapy encourages clients to create what he terms *sick imagery*. He thought that channeling disturbing emotional material into concrete artistic forms supports a lack of inner control for clients. We often debated whether expression or suppression of feelings was healthier for clients. I believe that expression is not harmful to people, but that keeping secrets and bottling up feelings is. My psychiatrist colleague viewed artistic imagery (at least that produced by psychiatric clients) as *pathological,* which means altered or brought on by disease. On the other hand, I asserted that artworks are expressions of *pathos,* which is an experience or element in artistic representation that evokes compassion.

The pathos-pathology polarity is a pivotal philosophic quandary for art therapists. This polarity encompasses the primary approaches to imagery that pervade the art therapy profession. A philosophic continuum between pathos and pathology allows for many ways to think about clients' images and artworks, and styles of relating with them. At one pole of the continuum is the pathologizing view of client artwork in which images are regarded as expressions of unconscious conflict and potential indicators of illness. Art therapists with a psychoanalytic or psychodynamic theoretical orientation often embrace this perspective. At the other pole of the continuum is the view that images are generated by pathos, and client' artworks are healthy intermediaries that carry messages to and from the self.

When clients' artworks are considered to be overt expressions of unconscious and conflicted psychic material, particular meanings can

159

be ascribed to the symbols presented. Typically in this model, images are regarded as servants of the *id,* and representations of powerful sexual and aggressive impulses and drives. Art therapists who subscribe to this style of relating to imagery may attempt to classify and catalogue images. These efforts inevitably lead to formulaic understandings of the meanings of images such as: *snakes = phallic symbols; caves = vaginal openings;* and *fires = rage.* Such formulas tend to focus on a disease orientation and dysfunctional aspects of clients. From this perspective, images are regarded as concrete representations of inner conflict.

Another offshoot to an approach that focuses on pathological understandings of art products suggests that clients with certain types of psychiatric disorders often create artworks that are emblematic of their disorder and similar enough to allow classification. This implies that art therapists who see the artwork of a given individual receive hints about the client's diagnosis. According to this logic, if an art therapist believed that clients with depression tend to choose black and blue paint, the art therapist might presume that the client was depressed based on color choice. A drawback of this approach is that one is seldomly diagnosed as being healthy and joyful. The process of diagnosis is reserved for those who already believe that something is wrong with them. In other words, to approach imagery from a diagnostician's perspective suggests that images are manifestations of disease or dysfunction.

At the other end of the philosophic continuum is the view that images are healthy expressions (Allen, 1992, 1995; McNiff, 1973, 1974, 1981, 1982, 1986, 1989, 1992; B. L. Moon, 1990, 1992, 1994, 1998, 2003, 2004, 2007). McNiff first articulated that images are message bearers, and though their messages may be disturbing, they are not destructive. He continues to champion the idea that images do not come to hurt or harm.

In the 1991 keynote address to the Buckeye Art Therapy Association annual symposium, McNiff told the story of a dream image painted by a student during a studio workshop. (He later wrote about this interchange in *Art as Medicine.*) The dream image was of a dark ninja who comes in the night and places a black net over the student's head. The student expressed fear and anxiety about the dream. Operating from the pathos perspective, McNiff suggested that perhaps the ninja was presenting itself in the dream to help the student get in touch with her feelings and turn off her intellectualizations. From this perspective, the ninja image that had been regarded as threatening could be viewed as a benevolent entity bearing an important message to the dreamer.

Over the years, in the art therapy studio and classroom, I have often encountered images that are simultaneously disturbing and instructive. One of my students struggled with images of boxes that repeatedly emerged in her drawings in client groups and her personal studio experiences. The box images initially seemed to represent the student's way of compartmentalizing various aspects of her life; the walling-off served a defensive and inhibiting function in the student's life. It was tempting to interpret the box images as symbolic of repressed, conflicted material, or indications of a dysfunctional aspect of the student's personality; instead, the student and I chose to regard the boxes as bearers of important messages. By establishing a creative dialogue and attending to the artworks in a respectful manner, we came to know the boxes as intriguing mysteries that invited the student to loosen her tight and constricting emotional controls. Over the course of her education, the sharp edges and harsh dividing lines softened.

I find it helpful to think of and relate to artworks and images as if they have a life of their own. For example, even though my own paintings are reflections of me, they are more than that. As evidence of an artwork's autonomy, I suggest gathering 10 friends and, independently of one another, asking them to tell a story about one of your artworks. I guarantee that 10 different stories will be recounted, each different from the story that you, the creator, would tell.

From this perspective, an image is not only an object of inquiry, but also a subject capable of teaching. If the image has a life and sovereignty of its own, we must regard our work as sacred because we deal with living images and the living artists who made them. Both subjects deserve respect. When artworks are respected, it is impossible to establish a formulaic approach to interpretation or equation for analysis because to do so would be analogous to performing an autopsy on the image. Autopsies are reserved for the dead. Artworks should not be seen as cadavers to be measured, labeled, and pathologized. In relation to clients' artworks and images, the reality is that *this* does not always mean *that*. In my work with the art of real-live clients, *2 + 2* often does not equal four. On the contrary, the world of imagination and art is full of mist and shadows that defy psychometrics and categorization. As art therapists, we embrace the mystery and cultivate *devotional seeing* (B. L. Moon, 1992). Our work often takes us into ambiguous worlds where nothing is absolute.

Art therapists can regard clients' artworks and images as either infectious and diseased, or compassionate messengers worthy of our most tender care and highest respect. The choice we make colors every aspect of our career because it affects how we relate to our clients, artworks, and ourselves. I urge compassion over dissection, and pathos over pathology.

Chapter 12

WHO, WHAT, WHERE,
WHEN, WHY, AND HOW

It is a tenet of journalism that good news stories include answers to the questions *who, what, where, when, why,* and *how.* In mystery novels, the task of the hero/detective is always to establish what the crime was, where and when it was committed, how it was done, why it was perpetrated, and who the culprit is. On television, lawyers doggedly gather facts relevant to their cases.

For journalists, detectives, and lawyers, interrogation is integral. Cross-examination and penetrating query are essential skills for Clark Kent, Dick Tracy, and Perry Mason. This is not the case, however, with art therapists; we are not in the business of investigating criminals or exposing unsavory details of a public figure's behavior. For art therapists, the image of an archaeologist patiently brushing away dust from the artifacts of some long past civilization is a better metaphor for our profession. The archaeologist seeks not to disturb, but to patiently and gently make visible.

In my work with students, I repeatedly tell them, "Create a dialogue with the client and the artwork, and don't interrogate." Cross-examination and interrogation are tactics of intrusion and manipulation. As art therapists, our effort must be toward encouraging the sharing of images in an atmosphere of mutual respect and honor.

Sentences that begin with *who, what, where, when, why,* and *how* set a tone of inquisition that is not conducive to sharing. These questions, as do those of the detective, seek objective facts. For example, in working with the client who painted Figure 18, an imaginal detective (the art therapist) might begin with an interchange like the following:

Figure 18. *Maplewood*–Acrylic on canvas.

Therapist: What is this building you have painted?
Client: I'm not sure.
Therapist: Who lives in this place? Who lives here?
Client: I really don't know.
Therapist: Do you have any idea where this building might be?
Client: No.
Therapist: When have you seen such a place?
Client: I'm not sure.
Therapist: Then why did you paint it?
Client: I don't know!

One can almost see the harsh light shining in the client's eyes. When an art therapist operates from this interrogative mode, little therapeutic work is done. When pushed with who, what, where, when, why, and how questions, clients tend to retreat into brief answers, and withdraw from the art therapist. The search for facts does little more than intimidate and alienate. I find it helpful to avoid the role of inquisitor when exploring artworks and images, whether they are those of clients, colleagues, or my own. How can this be done?

An Arts-based Alternative to Inquisition

I propose an arts-based model of engagement with clients' artworks and images. In an arts-based approach, the art therapist creates an imaginal dialogue with the stories of the artwork. The stories may be in the form of clients' narrative descriptions of the art, or they may emerge through a process of responsive art-making. Responsive art-making is a process that involves the artist/therapist creating artworks as a form of therapeutic intervention in response to the images of clients. This process helps art therapists in three ways: (1) as an aid in establishing empathic relationships; (2) as an expressive outlet for the art therapist's powerful feelings that are often stirred up in the clinical context; and (3) as the starting place for imaginative interpretive dialogue.

A number of authors have focused attention on the process of art therapists making art in the context of therapy, either during or post-session (Cohn, 1984; Haessler, 1989; Kielo, 1991; Lachman-Chapin, 1983; Robbins, 1988; Wolf, 1990). Responsive art-making refers to art that is created in the studio in the presence of the client that seeks to clarify feelings, explore levels of consciousness, and deepen relationships. Responsive art-making involves the artist/therapist in a form of creative therapeutic intervention in response to the images of clients that involves therapists' creative use of language, visual art skills, bodily movement, voice, and other modes of expression.

The following is an example of how I would use imaginal dialogue in relation to figure 18, and avoid the use of who, what, where, when, why, and how questions.

Bruce: I look at your painting and I can almost hear the wind rustling those curtains." Then I would make a low whistling sound, "Whoooooooo.

Client: I can feel it on my face.

Bruce: Something about your painting reminds me of a hot August afternoon.

Client: No, I was thinking of October. A cool, clear fall day.

Bruce: Fall is a time of change.

Client: Uh huh.

Bruce: I am drawn to the openings, the window and the door. They are inviting but also mysterious.

Client: Mysterious is a good word. It looks so dark in there. I think it's scary.

Bruce: I like the contrasts of the warm brown, stark white, and cool blue.

Client: That's me, all right. My friends say that I am hot and cold. I guess I can be moody.

Bruce: I feel a little lonely when I look at your painting.

Client: Yes.

Bruce: Sometimes people talk about houses and buildings as being symbols of themselves.

Client: I can sure relate to that.

In this brief interchange, rather than rely on who, what, where, when, why, and how questions, I used imaginal and sensual words. *Wind rustling, hot, fall, mysterious, warm, stark, cool,* and *wonder* are words that invite imaginative thinking and interaction. By using language in this manner, I enter a dialogue with the client and painting. The intent of the imaginal dialogue is not to categorize or label the image or client, but rather to be in relation with and understand. By using imaginal and sensual words, I honor the image-making process by responding to it on its own artistic terms.

Other ways that I could have responded to the painting in figure 18 include: (1) writing a poem about the building and its locale; (2) creating movement in response to the blowing curtains; (3) painting or drawing an image from the perspective of someone looking out at the world from behind the curtains; (4) viewing the painting as a scene in a movie, then creating an image of the next scene; (5) engaging the client in a dialogue about and appropriate sound track for the movie; and (6) imagining walking into the building and then portraying the interior.

In an art-based response to clients and their artworks, the effort is not to unearth the truth about images or their makers, but rather to help clients go deeper into the meanings of their artworks. A client's artwork inspires the art therapist's creative work, and the art therapist's responsive art encourages the client to make again. A creative reciprocity is thus established that honors both the images and artists.

As art therapists, it is a compliment to have the client leave our presence with a solid sense of having been respected. Neither do the criminal villain questioned by the detective nor the subject of the investigative reporter's queries feel respected.

Years ago, a student in the Harding Graduate Art Therapy Program came to supervision distraught. The student's on-site art therapy supervisor had remarked that responsive art-making was elitist. Her supervisor thought that attending to the image in an arts-based way was too time-consuming and indirect. She told the student that things must be put into words directly and quickly, and that engaging in responsive art-making and imaginal dialogue was impractical.

I responded: "If words are all that matter, perhaps your site supervisor is correct. However, there are many other disciplines whose main focus is cognitive discourse. I suggest that art therapists who long too strongly for things to be put into words are engaging in elitist mimicry of disciplines like psychiatry, psychology, social work, and counseling."

Art-making and imagery are the heart and soul of our professional identity. Our words must be used to honor and cherish images, not interrogate them. I encourage art therapists to avoid the who, what, where, when, why, and how mentality, and embrace an attitude of awe and wonder.

Chapter 13

THERAPEUTIC SELF

Since the beginning of civilization, people have sought the wisdom of a special few. S. Kopp (1971) refers to the special few as the *creative minority* whom others turn to for leadership, guidance, courage, understanding, and beauty.

As human beings, we vary from one another. Even members of the same family exhibit differences. Identical twins develop personality traits that set them apart from each other. Still, however, some qualities of human existence are common to us all. It can be argued that despite the diversity of our distinguishing characteristics, in the end, human similarities outnumber differences. All people, regardless of race, nationality, religion, socio-economic status, size, or shape enter the world as powerless, needing the good will and care of those around them to survive. Individuals must find their niche in the family or situation upon which they depend. All humans travel the difficult path from infancy through childhood, adolescence, adulthood, and old age.

As adults, we struggle with the joys and sorrows of finding companions. We form significant relationships, some of us raise children, and we all search for a sense of security and identity only to have it fade in later years. Ultimately, all people face death; the death of loved ones, friends, and inevitably ourselves is at the core of humankind's common experience of life.

Acknowledgment of the chaos and disquiet that accompany these common experiences causes each society to create systems, belief structures, rituals, and emissaries to support the journey of individual persons through the turbulence of life's passages. The profession of art therapy has developed metaverbal recognition of the way life is. In other times and places, shamans, witch doctors, clergy, and prophets filled this role. Art therapy is one of the current professions assigned to deal with the human struggle to survive and thrive.

From a theological standpoint, the therapeutic relationship may be described in the traditional terms of the ministerial roles of pastor, priest, and prophet. The pastor cares for, supports, consoles, and guides members of the congregation. The priest functions as the leader of sacred rituals that tell the essential story of the community through symbolic action language. The prophet reminds members of community of the way their lives are by focusing on the reality that by facing one's fears, meaning can be found.

As an art therapist, I find myself continually comforting my clients, engaging them in the rituals of creation in the studio and confronting their systems of denial about their lives. Art therapists engage in these tasks to establish therapeutic relationships. At times, our clients may see our work together as magical, drudgery, spiritual, supportive, challenging, comforting, or afflicting. All of these attributes share the common root that the therapeutic relationship is established for the sake of good healthy change and personal growth in clients. Each manifestation of our work is aimed toward relief of suffering, and each is effective when appropriately matched with the needs of the individual seeking service.

It is the art therapist's responsibility to see beyond conventional thought and trends of the present. We must understand that often what is hailed today as the latest wisdom offers only an illusory security. As art therapists, our historical connection to the role of the artist serves as the anchor for such creative courage. Artists of the world have always sought meanings that are deeper than fads, laws, and fashionable intellectual constructs. Documentation exists that artists frequently view the formalities of their particular era as little more than entertainment for the masses.

The art therapist must understand the unspoken language myths and dreams, which are metaphoric images that contain and express deep truths about the individual's life and the inner life of the surrounding culture. *Myth,* in this context, means the imaginal expression of humanity's most basic pleasures, struggles, and uncertainties. I do not use *myth* in the parochial sense of being a frivolous fiction. On the contrary, myths are the insights of the world, addressing foundational human experiences that have always been shared by people.

Dreams are to individuals what myths are to cultures. Dream images show truths about the dreamer's inner life. Although they may have little to do with fact, they always present truth in symbolic form.

Art therapists bring to the therapeutic relationship a deep respect for the unspoken language of dreams and myths. We do not translate or interpret them into rational constructs consistent with current thought. Rather, we kindle in our clients a respect for that which is not logical or sensible, yet still is true about themselves and their world. To do this, we must assure clients that images, whether dreamed or mythic, do not come to harm; rather, they come to enlighten.

Therapists, regardless of disciplinary tradition, are often described as charismatic. At the core of art therapists' charisma is an awareness of freedom that comes from artistic expression. Anything that can be painted can be reworked or painted over. It is impossible to predict what an artist will make next. The grace of our profession is nurtured through our capacity for innovation and undaunted fearlessness in the face of creative challenge.

Our artistic traditions allow us to be ultimately concerned with what we are doing at any given moment. At the same time, we must be content with doing only that which can be done. As painters build stretcher frames, they are not worried what the final picture will be. They must be satisfied with attending to construction. The charisma and grace of art therapists come from our capacity to trust the creative process and ourselves. Making art has taught us not to worry about how we are doing. We expect to sometimes feel lost, afraid, uncertain, and imperfect. When we embrace our fears and flaws, they no longer control us. Every time we face an empty canvas, we learn that nothing is certain; but if we trust the process and ourselves, the image will come. From these multiple experiences with media and work, we develop our capacity to console, lead, confront, and struggle.

All therapists must wrestle with difficult recurring questions regarding our level of transparency with our clients. What are our professional boundaries? What should we share about our lives with our clients? How closely should we guard our personal privacy? When and why do we share personal information with our clients? These questions and more swirl together and gradually come into focus on the issues of openness between art therapist and client.

In relation to the issue of art therapists' self-disclosure, there is a continuum ranging from complete opaqueness to transparency, with translucence approximately midway between:

OPAQUE	TRANSLUCENT	TRANSPARENT
All aspects of the art therapist's life are withheld from clients.	The art therapist is cautious about sharing personal information. The question is always asked, how will my sharing be helpful to clients?	The art therapy relationship is viewed as a mutual exhange of self-discovery between client and therapist.

Art therapists must decide for themselves where their therapeutic style falls on this continuum. When my students ask me for "the rules" regarding proper professional behavior in relation to self-disclosure, I tell them that they must experience the emptiness of a missed opportunity when they unnecessarily withhold information. Likewise, they must feel the pain of being abused by the client who was not ready or able to respond positively to the gift of the art therapist's vulnerability. These feelings must be experienced time and again to develop a set of inner cues that encourage discovery and warn to withhold when appropriate.

Regardless of the level of self-disclosure an art therapist chooses, it is essential that self-awareness (disclosure of the self to the self) remains a top priority. To maintain our authenticity as art therapists, we must be willing to constantly look in the creative mirror. We must see ourselves honestly. Sometimes, this is an easy process filled with excitement and joy, especially when we see images of courage and compassion. Other times, this is difficult, frightening, and overwhelming because reflections in the mirror may be ugly, grotesque, and disturbing. It is our strength, as artists, therapists, and art therapists to see our heroic and horrific, foolish and funny, and beautiful and beastly aspects. We can sometimes be opaque to our clients, but we can never be less than transparent to ourselves.

Finally, no discussion of therapeutic relationships is complete without the inclusion of love. Confrontation, consolation, struggle, charisma, and freedom are nothing without love. "And if I have prophetic powers, and understand all mysteries and all knowledge, and if I have all faith, so as to remove mountains, but have not love, I am nothing" (1 Corinthians 13:1–3).

It is not enough for an art therapist to be a gifted technician. It is not enough to understand the *Diagnostic and Statistical Manual of Mental Disorders,* developmental theories, or artistic techniques. The grace and charisma of art therapists cannot be used only to extol their own power and uniqueness. Art therapists' gifts find meaning only when they are used in the context of benevolent offerings of possibility to clients. To love is to maintain unselfish, loyal, and altruistic concern for the good of another. Making art is an act of love, as is providing therapy.

Chapter 14

ART THERAPISTS AND COLLEAGUES

Art therapists often find themselves working in treatment settings with a team of professional colleagues from other disciplines. Depending on the nature of the treatment facility, teams may consist of medical doctors, psychiatrists, psychologists, counselors, social workers, nurses, music therapists, dance/movement therapists, poetry therapists, drama therapists, occupational therapists, and any number of other related disciplines. The role of the art therapist in the team depends on the interplay between the leadership ability of the leader and the team abilities of the art therapist.

The ideal treatment team has a diverse range of talents, theoretical orientations, strengths, and points of view. The ideal team leader has the ability to set a tone of active inquiry based upon respect for the uniqueness and complexity of each client; respect for the professions and talents of individual team members; an ability to weave the threads of diverse information into a dynamic pattern that shows the individual client's situation; and an ability to motivate active team participation of all team members.

In the often hectic, verbal environment of team meetings, non-verbal therapies like art therapy can be overlooked. Art therapists must understand this challenge to becoming active and effective team members.

Huestis (as cited in B. L. Moon, 1994), a psychiatrist specializing in the care of adolescents at Riverside Methodist Hospital in Columbus, Ohio, describes his views about art therapists' contributions to psychiatric treatment teams: "My observation is that the effective team art therapist adapts along the lines of *thoughtful assertion* that has its own developmental phases. This development seems to be as predictable as physical development milestones in infants or the milestones in artistic evolution–random scribbling through early schema to naturalism and abstraction."

Development of the Team Art Therapist

In over fifteen years of observing and leading psychiatric treatment teams, I have noted that there is an evolutionary process that produces *thoughtful assertion.* The role that art therapists play on the team depends upon their evolutionary position. This is true for both experienced art therapists and novices. To illustrate: Imagine an "evolutionary tree." The trunk of this tree is a sense of professional security. That is the belief, fostered from both inside and outside experiences of the therapist, that the arts provide a unique piece of the therapeutic puzzle. The roots of the tree are the art processes themselves and the entire history of art. The art therapist who comes to team meetings with a secure sense of what art therapy is all about and how he or she relates to it has an enormous leg-up on being an effective member of the team. On the other hand, those who are caught in personal or professional identity crises and do not see themselves as truly equal with other disciplines tend to be timid members who don't venture forth with observations and interpretations when they are most needed, i.e., when the clinical picture is difficult to understand and the treatment process is stuck. A sense of personal security is especially important in art therapy, since its interventions are done non-verbally, while the rest of the mental health professions are so enamored of the spoken word. A secure person is much more likely to venture forth with a needed contribution.

A significant evolutionary branch is the ability to hold onto one's unique identity within a team structure. I have observed that the art therapist has a particularly difficult time with this, because the nature of mental health teams is so verbal and analytical while the art therapist's identity rests in the metaverbal or non-verbal Gestalt. The security to let art stand on its own seems to me to be a struggle throughout the art world. At a recent exhibit of George Bellows's work, I stood observing *Stag at Sharkey's.* I was aware of my inner experience of power, drama and struggle. The image stayed with me until I came to the end of the exhibit. There I was greeted with an overlay of the painting, with multiple lines "educating" me as to how the artist used a series of geometric triangles to create the picture. What a letdown! How quickly the former image and my former inner emotional experience faded!

Similarly, in teams I have seen powerful images and insights evaporate with excessive verbal analysis. The art therapist who is secure enough in his or her own identity to bring, share and educate members of the team with actual artistic productions of the client is a powerful advocate for the client and for the discipline. In short, use nonverbal pathways to emphasize the metaverbal nature of the art therapy experience.

At the same time that one is working on securing one's professional identity, the art therapist must strive to become a team player. If one expects the art therapy discipline to be respected, the art therapist must have respect for other professional disciplines and their interventions. It is important for the art therapist, who has a special power with clients who have some artistic interest, to reinforce the value of the other parts of the treatment plan that don't have an "artsy" flavor. For instance, one client on our adolescent unit was a fairly skilled artist, but he was so angry at his family that he refused to meet with them and the social worker for scheduled sessions. This went on for several weeks. The art therapist working with the client served as a gentle persuader, subtly supporting the need to work things out with his parents, in the same way the client was able to work through difficult design problems in his painting. The art therapist pointed out that the client did not let his anger keep him away from the studio, nor should it keep him out of the family therapy session.

As the leader of the treatment team, how do I know I have team players? One of the surest ways is to ask the *client* about how confidentiality works on his team. If the client understands that he is covered by team confidentiality, I know he is surrounded by team players. Team confidentiality means that the client understands that what he produces in any therapeutic activity will be shared with all team members, but will not go outside the team. There is always the temptation to view one's work as just a little more important than someone else's. Professional pride is good, but when it leads to "special deals" between client and staff, it is destructive. All special deals backfire because they involve holding back clinical/milieu material. Holding back information quickly labels one as a non-team player. Because of the highly individualistic nature of artistic production, I have seen beginning art therapists struggle with sharing therapeutic information with other team members. It is a constant struggle with clients to make it clear that, while artistic production is individualistic, keeping part or all of the artistic experience outside the team is a blueprint for therapeutic trouble and team alienation.

This idea of sharing information also applies to information that might be "different" from what other team members are reporting—that your interaction with the client is not the same as theirs. It may be positive, e.g., that in art therapy groups he isn't obnoxious, hard to engage or unwilling to share. Oftentimes there is the tendency to withhold negative material, out of fear that it will personally reflect on you or your ability as a therapist. Once your professional identity is secure, it will be easier to see that to a well-functioning team, it is just as important to know who isn't working in an activity, who is making personal attacks on the therapist, or who is devaluing any part of their treatment program.

The therapist who reports only successes and triumphs and no personal discomfort is suspect as a team player.

The mental set that is most helpful in team meetings is a respect for different views of the same client. Differences are interesting. There would be no need to have team meetings if everyone was going to say the same thing. The best therapists and team leaders can tolerate some ambiguity and wait for the picture to unfold, much like an artist must tolerate not knowing how a painting will end up.

Another important branch in the development of thoughtful assertion is knowing what kinds of individuals will benefit most from art therapy activities as well as when to initiate them. As one builds an identity, these kinds of decisions should become easier, as long as the art therapist is guarding against his own complacency: engaging only those individuals that make him feel comfortable and avoiding those clients that challenge him or stimulate unpleasant affect.

This is a complicated matter, for on the one hand it might be argued that the process of making art is intrinsically therapeutic for all persons. However, in the setting of the psychiatric institution, often operating under constraints of time and resources, it is essential that therapeutic interventions be made in a way that is efficient, both psychologically and fiscally.

The art therapist must develop a sense of who he works most efficiently with. At the same time he must not be so narrow in self-evaluation of efficacy as to exclude groupings of clients with whom he has had little or no experience. It is perfectly natural that, early in their careers, art therapists will be drawn to clients who share their interest in art. In a sense, such clients mirror the values of the novice therapist, making interaction both pleasant and meaningful. As the art therapist matures, less of this mirroring quality is required. The professional challenge to the developing art therapist is to gradually expand the variety of clients he or she can work with effectively. Eventually, one's professional competence includes clients who may openly state that they detest art.

Two key aspects of this evolutionary process are honesty and confidence. You must be honest enough in a team setting to speak up when you feel you cannot handle working with a given client. There is nothing wrong in knowing and sharing your limitations. On the contrary, damage can be done if you allow yourself to overextend your competency. Likewise, you must develop confidence in your own strengths. It is inappropriate to accept only those clients who reflect your interests and values. It is crucial that art therapy students and novice practitioners not expect themselves to be experts on the first day of their professional life (pp. 177–181).

Art and the Milieu

There are a number of indirect ways that art therapists can educate members of a treatment team and enhance the treatment milieu. One way is to bring client artwork to team meetings. Another way is to encourage the ethical use of client art in the decor of the inpatient living areas. When I worked at Harding Hospital, the atmosphere of the living units was enriched when the art pieces selected by an interior designer were replaced with clients' artworks. This gave a potent metaverbal message that the hospital was a place where clients matter and their work is appreciated.

There was a related phenomenon of clients giving pieces of artwork to the unit at the time of their discharge. This became fairly common and pushed the treatment team to think about the meaning of the gifts. Four distinct motivations were identified:

1. *Affirmation*–Departing clients wanted to demonstrate to the unit staff their positive feelings about the therapy experience. Leaving

behind a "good-bye painting" was an affirmation of the client's positive regard for the treatment process.

2. *The Closet Effect*–When older adolescents move out of their parents' home, whether to go to college or an apartment of their own, they often leave behind personal belongings in the closets. Conscious or not, this has the effect of leaving a part of themselves in the safety of parental care. The closet effect of the departing client serves the same purpose, i.e., symbolically maintaining a connection to the safe, nurturing, and predictable treatment milieu.

3. *Giving Back*–Often terminating clients long to give back a part themselves to the treatment team. This honors the giving that the staff has done during hospitalization.

4. *Concretization of Introject Exchange*–Most subtle is the idea that leaving an object of art behind represents a concretization of the exchange of introjects which has occurred within the client during the treatment process. When clients are first admitted, it is assumed that their self-view is negative. They have had countless interchanges over time that have solidified a negative self-concept. A major purpose of hospital treatment is to provide clients with many experiences with both neutral and positive emotional undertones. This is done through encounters with treatment personnel. Gradually, clients begin to reshape their sense of self as they experience healthy interchanges with the staff. In short, an exchange of introjects occurs. The leaving behind of the artwork becomes a concrete symbol of this process. The metaphoric message from the client is: "You knew me when I was bad, yet you stuck with me. Now that I feel better about myself, I want to leave this symbolic object behind as testimony to the work we did." (Huestis, as cited in B. L. Moon, 1994, pp. 184–185)

Chapter 15

OTHER CONSIDERATIONS

As I near the completion of this book in the midsummer of 2007, it is an intriguing time in the history of health care professions. Art therapy is not immune to the economic pressures that have adversely affected health care services in the United States. In 1993, the original version of this chapter was titled *Things To Worry About.* In the early '90s, some art therapy educational programs closed their doors because of insufficient funding. At the same time, radical shifts in the insurance industry resulted in drastic changes in health care service-delivery systems. Those changes, coupled with the deinstitutionalization movement, caused significant downsizing, and sometimes closure of private and state hospitals.

In the ensuing years, health care in the United States has become a political hot potato that neither democrats nor republicans seem to be able to cool. In addition, technological advances spur ever-rising health care costs that shrink the accessibility to care for millions of underinsured and uninsured people. The well-being of clients has been reduced to concrete measures in dollars and cents. Treatment of chronic illness, whether psychic or somatic, has been labeled as a bad investment, and resources have been allocated elsewhere.

Despite the economic trauma that has afflicted the health care industry, art therapy continues to grow in demand and popularity. It is common for art therapists to work independently of the established and ailing health care institutions. More and more, art therapists are establishing private practices and successfully competing with other helping professions. This is happening partly out of necessity and partly in response to demand from the consumer.

Perils of Success

Although the art therapy profession now requires a master's degree, many art therapists find themselves surrounded in the workplace by bachelor's level colleagues early in their careers. For example, music therapists, horticulture therapists, recreation therapists, and until recently occupational therapists do not have master's level educational requirements. Thus, art therapists are often prematurely promoted to positions of clinical supervisor or program director because of their advanced educational experience.

On the surface, promotion is attractive to a young therapist because it means more money, prestige, and political and programmatic power within the treatment system. When one is offered more money, freedom, and control, the temptation is strong to accept the promotion without question. There is, however, a darker side: Promotion usually brings an increase in pressure, responsibilities for documentation, and administrative demands, accompanied by a decrease in client contact, studio art time, and contact with peers who are now supervisees or employees. Factors that motivated the art therapy novice to seek the profession, such as a belief in the essential goodness of art-making processes, a desire to use the arts as a means of helping humanity, and a genuine longing to make a difference in the world, can be easily subverted by the lure of earning power, ego inflation, and control domination.

While it is not impossible for art therapists to become clinical supervisors or program directors and remain true to their original intentions, it is easy for these motivations to get lost in the shuffle. The heart and soul of the art therapy profession is found in the contexts of the art therapy studio and therapeutic relationship. I've found that these qualities are often absent from the offices and job descriptions of program directors and clinical supervisors. These are not bad people who intentionally pulled away from their professional foundation; rather, the pressures of administration and supervision subtly and covertly deadened a part of their creative spirit. I have known art therapists who have lost their way so gradually that it is impossible to pinpoint when or what precipitated their lost-ness. It is, like trying to mark the exact spot where fog begins or ends, nearly impossible and probably irrelevant.

Occasionally, I have offered solace to colleagues when they have sought my advice on this topic. My suggestion is always the same, "Go into your studio and paint about this." The intent of these words is to encourage my colleagues to go to their source, listen to their own creativity, and seek their own solutions to dilemmas they face.

I think about this not only from the abstract position of the detached observer, but as one who has also wrestled with these issues in my own career. There was a period of time in my professional life when I was off track. Seduced by title and authority, I cut myself off from the phenomena that captured my heart and imagination decades prior. It was serendipitous that an arts experience reminded me of how and why I became an art therapist in the first place. I came into the field not expecting to become wealthy, not longing to be the boss, not wanting to spend my days behind a desk filling out evaluation forms, and disinterested in the business of mental health care. Rather, I came to the profession out of love, creative energy, and an internal drive to connect with fellow human beings through art. I was fortunate that I was in a position to extricate myself from the energy draining and creativity sapping aspects of my work. I was able to give up my desire for control and clout in exchange for professional integrity.

Security, Sanctity, and Alphabet Soup

There is a brief line of dialogue in the film *Why Man Creates* (Bass, 1968) that expresses the notion that all radical ideas eventually become institutions that reject new radical ideas. Half a century ago, art therapy was a radical new idea. In the ensuing years, the profession has done much to institutionalize itself. Rigorous standards of art therapy education have been established. Strict registration and arduous certification credentialing systems have been devised. The Art Therapy Credentials Board (ATCB) has developed and administers a national examination. The AATA governs and nurtures the development of the profession on a national scale. A demanding process of educational program approval has been instituted, and ethical principles of client care are endorsed by the AATA membership. The profession of art therapy has become an institution.

A disturbing aspect of the formalizing of the discipline is a trend toward uniformity of theory, philosophy, and approach. As the profession has become more clearly defined, there is tremendous temptation to insist on a narrow set of common understandings. This is a disturbing trend for it severs our connection with our own history and roots.

The pioneers who forged the earliest identity of art therapy in the United States came from a variety of educational, philosophical, and experiential backgrounds. Some came from psychology and psychiatry. Others found their way into the infant field by way of professional art, while still others came via ministry. It is evident that some of art therapy's founding fathers and mothers would qualify for entry into the profession under today's standards. This is inevitable and yet distressing.

The art therapy profession has been institutionalized to establish professional respectability and security. While there is nothing inherently wrong with respectability and security, the potential side effects have a malignant tone. Theoreticians who have strayed outside the mainstream of thought have found themselves to be the target of criticism from without, and within, the profession. An examination of published reviews of art therapy literature, written by art therapists, confirms that we are not always kind to one another. When we come together at our annual national conference, there is almost always an undertone of philosophic warfare.

I want to go on record here that while I passionately believe every word that I have written in this book, I hold no illusions that my way is the only way to practice art therapy. It is just my way. The ideas presented in this book are representative of one way to do the work. It is a good way, I think, but only one of many good ways. Just as abstract expressionists are no less artists than the surrealists, the primitives, the minimalists, the impressionists, or the post-modernists, so too are the psychodynamic art therapy theorists no less art therapists than the gestalt art therapists, the existential art therapists, the behavioral art therapists, the art-based art therapists, or the eclectic art therapists. To drive across the United States from east to the west coast, one can choose from many different roads and routes to reach a desired destination.

The sanctity of the art therapy profession ultimately is tied to our capacity to embrace difference. The first word of our disciplinary name, *art,* denotes a willingness to incorporate contrast and diversity into the "big picture." This is what artists have done from the beginning of time. If the measure of a fine mind is the capacity to hold two opposing ideas as true, then surely it is the sacred task of the individual art therapist and the institutions of art therapy alike to respect the possibility of multiple truths about this profession.

Some art therapists believe that the profession should align itself with the counseling profession. Some art therapists assert that to survive, the art therapy profession must assimilate the style of other professions and seek the credentials of those professions. This has resulted in a plethora of initials after art therapists' names. Among these credential letters are: LPAT, LPC, LPCC, LCPC, NCC, LMHC, MFCC, MFT, LMFT, MSW, LCSW, RPT, RPT-S, ATH-BC and Ph.D.–alphabet soup. Others insist that aligning with counseling or any other profession would result in a loss of disciplinary identity. Some art therapists believe we must participate in the political process of lobbying congress to be recognized in national legislation. Some art therapists think that obtaining a professional license is essential to their survival, whereas others view licensure as an irrelevant annoyance. Some see the future of art therapy depending upon validation from quantifiable research, whereas others call for research that is indigenous to art processes. I see all of these issues as signs that art therapy is vital, contentious, alive, and well.

Chapter 16

NOWHERE TO HIDE

If it is true that artists attempt to show us the world as it really is, then a primary task of art therapists is to engage with people without the aid of disguises or make-up. We must allow ourselves to be who we are without guile or manipulative intent. We must make our art in the company of clients as we encourage them to make theirs. As we look for the unique and authentic selves of our clients that have often been scarred or hidden deep within, we cannot help but encounter our own disfigurements and concealed facets. I have often wondered if this is why many art therapists cease to function as artists outside the confines of the work environment. So much energy is spent in the therapeutic context that it may seem daunting to explore one's own caverns continually.

As I mentioned earlier in this book, we Westerners have become comfortable with portraits of ourselves created in the darkrooms of the studio photographer. Pleasant backdrops, filtered lenses, warm light, and retouching techniques provide us with pictures of the selves we wish we were: no pimples, scars, or wrinkles. These unauthentic portraits have become the norm. But artists do dare to paint reality, and whether artworks are representational or abstract, they show us ourselves as we really are.

I believe that art should depict what is real and genuine about life. All art has an existential quality. When I had just finished my first book *Existential Art Therapy: The Canvas Mirror,* McNiff commented that the title was redundant. He said, "Everything about art is existential, and everything about existentialism is art." The aim of art and art therapy is to get beneath the surface of things, and once there, to use the gentle touch of the archaeologist to brush away the emotional debris of life and make room for more life. Scientists theorize and prove the way things are, whereas artists express the way things feel. Facts are irrelevant if the images and feelings associated with them are true.

Artists give the world pictures of what it means to be alive in a certain time and place. The anguish, vitality, and turbulent intensity of existence is essential to inquiry for art therapy.

As a practicing artist, my work has comforted me in times of stress and afflicted me in times of comfort. Sometimes I look at my paintings, and I am caught off guard by the courage and integrity I see. Other moments, I am sickened by the oozing, pus-filled open wounds haunted by loneliness and embarrassed by the cowardice I see. The dilemma I face as both an artist and existential art therapist is that I cannot run from the anguish these images bring me. I've tried, but it doesn't work. The faster I run, the quicker I am overtaken by the reality of my creation. There is no escape.

As I form these words on the screen of my computer, they inevitably fail to convey the depth of my passion for this profession. In the process of writing or reading a book, one is ultimately left in shallow regions. Art and art therapy are not subjects of academic investigation alone. One must make art and do art therapy to really understand this *Introduction to Art Therapy.*

I hope that the stories and ideas I have shared pique your interest. If I have done this with skill and integrity, perhaps you will be drawn into the profession the way I was 33 years ago. I feel grateful to the art therapists of a generation ago: those who pioneered the field, breathed life into the national association, and struggled to define a new and radical (yet old and proven) idea that making art is healthy. Without Jones, Naumburg, Kramer, Cohen, Ault, Levick, Stone, Ulman, Garai, Rhyne, Huntoon, Levy, and many others, it is probable that my life would have taken a different direction.

I also feel responsible to art therapists yet to come. In every circumstance of my professional life, I am cognizant that I am forced to choose my roads carefully, not only for my own well-being, but also for the sake of others. As an existential art therapist, I am constantly in the company of the artworks of my clients, colleagues, and students. The entire focus of these encounters is the mutual growth made possible through shared imaginal experiences.

As an art therapy educator, I am attentive to the images that emerge as my students progress in their educational process. I want to help students deepen and broaden their understanding of themselves as artists/therapists. The students' images invariably depict their processes of coming to grips with the angst they experience as they move from novice to graduate. I try always to be present and open to them as we meet to reflect on their experience of themselves as artists/therapists.

As I work on my paintings, I feel responsible to the art and myself. I paint in the company of my clients and colleagues, but still the making of art is ultimately solitary. As I stand before the blank canvas, I am aware of my aloneness. The tightly stretched canvas surface is not only an objective thing to be addressed, but also an inner reality. It calls to me to free it from its empty blankness. As my brush moves across the canvas, something deep within me vibrates and trembles. I believe that it is imperative that art therapists remain active artistically if they are to have any connection to the soul of the profession. If you are not committed equally to making art and serving humanity, choose another path for your life.

I regard the work that I do as sacred. Every time clients dip a wound in acrylic paint or dust it with chalk, they receive the nourishment and courage that their life journey demands. The therapy is not found in helping the client rise above suffering; rather, it is found in knowing how and when to immerse oneself in the creative flow.

My belief in the power and goodness of the art-making process is contagious. I don't have to tell my clients or students that I have faith in this. It oozes from my skin and is exhaled in the air I breathe. They see my faith with their own eyes. I don't have to talk about my concern that art therapists should remain active artistically. They smell my sweat and see my commitment. Students, clients, and colleagues alike do not have to fear that I will leave them stranded in the midst of their journey. I will stand with them and welcome them in the studio. Together, we will make art.

"Walk with me," I tell them. "Let us baptize our wounds in paint and draw the strength and courage we need to continue our journeys. We have nothing and nowhere to hide."

Figure 19. *Kneeling Figures*–Oil Stik on masonite.

EPILOGUE

It is presumptuous to expect that this book has completely introduced the complex and diverse field of art therapy as it is now practiced in the United States. Still, the act of presuming is an act of imagination, so I pretend that I have adequately created a text that touches the major themes and issues of the art therapy profession.

I hope that this book will be among the first ones read by students new to the field. The strengths of this text are in its constant reference to art-making processes and human compassion. It is my desire that readers finish this book with a good feeling about the discipline. I picture them laying the book down and saying, "Art therapy is a humane field that is ultimately concerned with love, artworks, and images." If this is the case, then I have been successful in creating the introduction I set out to make.

Note that there are shortcomings to this book. I do not acquaint the reader with theories of symbolic interpretation because I cannot (and will not) write what I do not believe. Nor do I provide information on the scientific use of art as therapy. There are also client populations that I have not attempted to addressed, including developmentally challenged persons, persons with AIDS, or the hearing-impaired. Although I have provided clinical art therapy services to each of these populations, I chose examples that I find applicable to a wider spectrum of people. I will leave the writing of art therapy books for particular diagnostic categories to others in the profession; the core of the work is the same.

Our journey through this book is nearly complete. We have traveled a highway adorned with images, blood, metaphor, passion, and mystery. I hope you have enjoyed the ride, and I pray that you have felt the joy and passion that I have for the work. I feel blessed to have come upon the profession of art therapy. Even after three decades, each Monday morning I look forward to getting out of bed and going to work. I love what I do, and I would likely do it as a volunteer were I not fortunate enough to be paid for my labor.

I have attempted to present the essence of the art therapy profession as faithfully as I can. Our roots lay in two continents: the land of art and the land of therapy. We must always straddle the intercontinental divide with care and balance. We must always make art, and we must always love. This is art therapy.

Peace,

Bruce L. Moon

REFERENCES

Adler, A. (1958). *What life should mean to you.* New York: Capricorn (Original work published 1931).

Allen, P. B. (1995). *Art is a way of knowing: A guide to self-knowledge and spiritual fulfillment through creativity.* Boston: Shambhala.

Allen, P. B. (1992). Artist-in-residence: An alternative to "clinification" for art therapists. *Art Therapy: Journal of the American Art Therapy Association, 9*(1), 22–9.

Alter-Muri, S. (1998). Texture in the melting pot: Postmodernist art and art therapy. *Art Therapy: Journal of the American Art Therapy Association, 15* (4), 245–251.

American Art Therapy Association. (2003). *Ethical principles for art therapists.* Mundelein, IL: American Art Therapy Association.

American Psychiatric Association. (2000). *Diagnostic and statistical manual of mental disorders* (text rev.). Washington, D.C.: Author.

Ault, R. (1977). Are you an artist or a therapist: A professional dilemma of art therapists. In R. Shoemaker & S. Gonnick-Barris (Eds.), *Proceedings of the 7th Annual American Art Therapy Association Conference* (pp. 55–56). Baltimore: American Art Therapy Association.

Bass, S. (1968). *Why man creates* [Film/video]. Santa Monica, CA: Pyramid Films.

Belkofer, C. (2003). *A new kind of wonder: Art therapy and neuroscience.* Unpublished master's thesis, School of the Art Institute of Chicago, Chicago.

Bly, R. (1990). *Iron John: A book about men.* New York: Addison-Wesley.

Boston, C. (2006). Notes: Georgette Seabrook Powell. *Art Therapy: Journal of the American Art Therapy Association, 23*(2), 89.

Cohn, R. (1984). Resolving issues of separation through art. *The Arts in Psychotherapy, 11,* 29–35.

Collins, J. (1972) My father. On *Who knows where the time goes* [LP]. New York: Elektra Records.

Corey, G. (2005). *Theories and techniques of counseling.* Belmont, CA: Brooks/Cole.

DeBrular, D. (1988). *Spirituality and the arts.* Paper presented at the annual conference held at Ursuline College, Cleveland, OH.

Doby-Copeland, C. (2007). Things come to me: Reflections from an art therapist of color. *Art Therapy: Journal of the American Art Therapy Association, 23*(2), 81–85.

Elkins, D. E., Stovall, K., & Malchiodi, C. (2003). American Art Therapy Association, Inc.: 2001–2002 membership survey report. *Art Therapy: Journal of the American Art Therapy Association, 20* (1), 28–34.

191

Ellis, A. (1993). *Fundamentals of rational-emotive therapy*. In W. Dryden, & L. K. Hill (Eds.), *Innovations in rational-emotive therapy* (pp. 1–32). Newbury Park, CA: Sage.

Ewens, T. (1988). Flawed understandings: On Getty, Eisner and dbae. In J. Burton, A. Lederman,& P. London (Eds.). *Beyond dbae: The case for multiple visions of art education*. North Dartmouth: Southeastern Massachusetts University.

Farris, P. (2006). Mentors of diversity: A tribute. *Art Therapy: Journal of the American Art Therapy Association, 23*(2), 86–88.

Feen-Calligan, H., & Sands-Goldstein, M. (1996). A picture of our beginnings: The artwork of art therapy pioneers. *American Journal of Art Therapy, 35,* 43–53.

Felshin, N. (Ed.). (1995). *But is it art?: The spirit of art as activism*. Seattle, WA: Bay Press.

Fleming, M. (1993). From clinician to artist; From artist to clinician, part I: A personal account. *American Journal of Art Therapy, 31*(3), 70–75.

Frankl, V. E. (1969). *Man's search for meaning: An introduction to logotherapy*. Philadelphia: Washington Square Press.

Franklin, M., Farelly-Hansen, M., Marek, B., Swan-Foster, N., & Wallingford, S. (2000). Transpersonal art therapy education. *Art Therapy: Journal of the American Art Therapy Association, 17*(2), 101–110.

Fromm, E. (1955). *The sane society*. New York: Fawcett World Library.

Fromm, E. (1956). *The art of loving*. New York: Harper & Row.

Haeseler, M. (1989). Should art therapists create art alongside their clients? *American Journal of Art Therapy, 27,* 70–79.

Haley, J. (1973). *Uncommon therapy: The psychiatric techniques of Milton H. Erikson, M.D.* New York: Norton.

Hamburg, D.A. (1963). Emotions in perspective of human evolution. *Expressions of Emotions of Man*. Symposium held at the meeting of the American Association for the Advancement of Science in New York on December 29–30, 1960 (Unknown Binding) P. Knapp, ed. New York: International Universities Press.

Harvey, V. (1971). *A handbook of theological terms*. New York: The Macmillan Company.

Henley, D. (1992). Aesthetics in art therapy: Theory into practice. *The Arts in Psychotherapy, 19*(3),   153–61.

Hillman, J. (1989). *A blue fire*. New York: Harper & Row.

Hogan, S. (1997). *Feminist approaches to art therapy*. London: Routledge.

Horovitz, E. G. (1994). *Spiritual art therapy: An alternate path*. Springfield, IL: Charles C Thomas.

Horovitz-Darby, E. G. (1999). *A leap of faith: The call to art*. Springfield, IL: Charles C Thomas.

Huestis, R., Ryland, C. (1990). Outcome after partial-hospital treatment of severely disturbed adolescents. *International Journal of Partial Hospitalization, 6*(2).

Jagger, M., & Richards, K. (1969). You can't always get what you want. On *Let it bleed* [LP]. New York: ABKCO Records.

Jones, D. (1980). *Draw from within* [Video]. Worthington, OH. Author.

Jones, D. (1974). *Some assumptions about the therapeutic use of art*. Unpublished manuscript.

Junge, M., B., & Asawa, P. P. (1994). *A history of art therapy in the United States.* Mundelein, IL: American Art Therapy Association.

Kapitan, L. (1998). In pursuit of the irresistible: Art therapy research in the hunting tradition. *Art Therapy: Journal of the American Art Therapy Association, 17*(2), 111–117.

Kaplan, F. (2000). *Art, science and art therapy: Repainting the picture.* Philadelphia: Jessica Kingsley.

Kielo, J. (1991). Art therapist's countertransference and post-session therapy imagery. *Art Therapy: The Journal of the American Art Therapy Association, 8*(2), 14–19.

Kopp, S. B. (1971). Guru; Metaphors from a psychotherapist. Palo Alto, CA: Science and Behavior Books.

Kopp, R. R. (1995). *Metaphor therapy: Using client-generated metaphors in psychotherapy.* New York: Brunner/Mazel.

Kramer, E. (1971/1993). *Art as therapy with children.* New York: Schocken Books. (reprinted 1993, Chicago: Magnolia St.).

Kramer, E., & Wilson L. (1979). *Childhood and art therapy: Notes on theory and application.* New York: Schocken.

Lachman-Chapin, M. (1983). The artist as clinician: An interactive technique in art therapy. *American Journal of Art Therapy, 23,* 13–25.

Lachman-Chapin, M. (1993). From clinician to artist; From artist to clinician, part II: Another perspective. *American Journal of Art Therapy, 31*(3), 76–80.

Lachman-Chapin, M. (1994). *Reverberations: Mothers & daughters.* Evanston, IL: Evanston Publishing.

Lacy, S. (Ed.). (1995). *Mapping the terrain: New genre public art.* Seattle, WA: Bay Press.

Lattanzi-Licht, M. & Doka, K. J. (Eds.). (2003). *Living with grief: Coping with public tragedy.* NY: Brunner-Routledge-Hospice Foundation of America.

Levick, M. F. (1983). *They could not talk and so they drew: Children's styles of coping and thinking.* Springfield, IL: Charles C Thomas.

Levick, M. F., & Wheeler, D. S. (1986). *Mommy, daddy, look what I'm saying: What children are telling you through their art.* New York: M. Evans.

Levine, S. K., & Levine, E. G. (1999). *Foundations of expressive arts therapy: Theoretical and clinical perspectives.* London: Jessica Kingsley.

Levine, S. K. (1992). *Poiesis: The language of psychology and the speech of the soul.* Toronto, Canada: Palmerston Press.

Lusebrink, V. B. (1990). *Imagery and visual expression in therapy (Emotions, personality, and psychotherapy).* New York: Plenum Press.

Malchiodi, C. A. (2003). *Handbook of art therapy.* New York: Guilford Press.

Maslow, A. H. (1968). *Toward a psychology of being.* New York: Van Nostrand Reinhold.

Maslow, A. H. (1975). *The farther reaches of human nature.* New York: Viking.

May, R. (1975). *The courage to create.* New York: W.W. Norton.

McLean, D. (1971). American Pie. On *American pie* [LP]. New York: United Artists Records.

McNiff, S. (1973). A new perspective in group art therapy. *Art Psychotherapy 1,* 3–4.

McNiff, S. (1974). Organizing visual perception through art. *Academic Therapy, 9*(6).

McNiff, S. (1981). *The arts and psychotherapy.* Springfield, IL: Charles C Thomas.

McNiff, S. (1982). Working with everything we have. *American Journal of Art Therapy, 21,* 4.

McNiff, S. (1986). *Fundamentals of art therapy.* Springfield, IL: Charles C Thomas.

McNiff, S. (1989). *Depth psychology of art.* Springfield, IL: Charles C Thomas.

McNiff, S. (1992). *Art as medicine.* Boston: Shambhala.

McNiff, S. (1995). Keeping the studio. *Art Therapy: Journal of the American Art Therapy Association. 12,* 182.

McNiff, S. (1998). *Art-based research.* London: Jessica Kingsley.

McNiff, S. (2004). *Art heals: How creativity cures the soul.* Boston: Shambhala.

Menninger, K. (1942). *Love against hate.* New York: Harcourt, Brace and World.

Mills, J. C., & Crowley, R. J. (with Ryan, M. O.). (1986). *Therapeutic metaphors for children and   the child within.* New York: Brunner/Mazel.

Moon, B. L. (1990, 1995). *Existential art therapy: The canvas mirror.* Springfield, IL: Charles C Thomas.

Moon, B. L. (1992, 2003). *Essentials of art therapy education and practice.* Springfield, IL: Charles C Thomas.

Moon, B. L. (1994). *Introduction to art therapy: Faith in the product.* Springfield, IL: Charles C Thomas.

Moon, B. L. (1998). *The dynamics of art as therapy with adolescents.* Springfield, IL: Charles C Thomas.

Moon, B. L. (1999). The tears made me paint. *Art Therapy: Journal of the American Art Therapy Association, 16*(2).

Moon, B. L. (1996, 2004). *Art and Soul: Reflections on an Artistic Psychology* (2nd ed.). Springfield, IL: Charles C Thomas.

Moon, B. L. (2002). *The acoustic memory project.* Proceedings of the National Conference of the American Art Therapy Association, Washington, D.C.

Moon, B. L. (2007). *The role of metaphor in art therapy: Theory, method, and experience.* Springfield, IL: Charles C Thomas.

Moon, C. H. (1989). *Art as prayer.* Proceedings of the National Conference of the American Art Therapy Association, San Francisco.

Moon, C. H. (2000). Art therapy, profession or idea? A feminist aesthetic perspective. *Art Therapy: Journal of the American Art Therapy Association, 17*(1), 7–10.

Moon, C. H. (2001). Prayer, sacrament, and grace. In M. Farelly-Hansen (Ed.), *Spirituality and art therapy: Living the connection.* London: Jessica Kingsley.

Moon, C. H. (2002). *Studio art therapy: Cultivating the artist identity in the art therapist.* London: Jessica Kingsley.

Moore, M. (2001). *Stupid white men.* New York: Harper Collins.

Moustakas, C. E. (1994). *Existential psychotherapy and the interpretation of dreams.* New York: Jason Aronson.

Naumburg, M. (1947/1973). Studies of the free art expression of behavior problem children &   adolescents as a means of diagnosis and therapy. *Nervous & Mental Disorders Monograph.* No. 71. (Reprinted as *Introduction to art therapy,* 1973, New York: College Press.)

Naumburg, M. (1966). *Dynamically oriented art therapy: Its principles and practice.* New

York: Grune and Stratton.

Papini, G. (1934). A visit to Freud. *Colosseum.* Reprinted in *Rev. Existential Psychology and Psychiatry IX* (1969): 130–34.

Perls, F. (1969). *Gestalt therapy verbatim.* Moab, UT: Real People Pess.

Pirsig, R. M. (1974). *Zen and the art of motorcycle maintenance: An inquiry into values.* New York: Bantam Books.

Rhyne, J. (1973). *The gestalt art experience.* Monterey, CA: Brooks/Cole Publishing (2nded. 1995, Magnolia St.).

Rhyne, J. (1995). *The gestalt art experience.* (2nd ed.). Chicago: Magnolia Street Publishers.

Richter, J. P., (Writer), & M. Hale (Trans.). (1973). *Horn of Oberon: Jean Paul Richter's school for aesthetics.* Detroit, MI: Wayne State University Press. (Original work published in 1804.)

Riley, S. (1999). *Contemporary art therapy with adolescents.* Philadelphia: Jessica Kingsley .

Riley, S., & Malchiodi, C. A. (1994). *Integrative approaches to family art therapy.* Chicago: Magnolia Street Publishers.

Robbins, A. (1987). *The artist as therapist.* New York: Human Services Press.

Robbins, A. (1988). A psychoaesthetic perspective on creative arts therapy and training. *The Arts in Psychotherapy, 15,* 95–100.

Robbins, A. (2001). Object relations and art therapy. In J. A. Rubin (Ed.), *Approaches to art therapy* (2nd ed., pp. 54–65). New York: Brunner-Routledge.

Rogers, C. R. (1951). *Client-centered therapy: Its current practices, implications and theory.* New York: Houghton Mifflin.

Rogers, C. R. (1961). *On becoming a person: A therapist's view of psychotherapy.* Boston: Houghton Mifflin.

Rubin, J. A. (1999). *Art therapy: An introduction.* Philadelphia: Brunner/Mazel.

Silverstone, L. (1997). *Art therapy the person-centered way: Art and the development of the person* (2nd ed.). London: Jessica Kingsley.

Simon, P. (1983). Train in the distance. On *Hearts and bones* [LP}. New York: Warner Brothers.

Talbott-Green, M. (1989). Feminist scholarship: Spitting into the mouths of the gods. *The Arts in Psychotherapy, 16,* 253–261.

Timm-Bottos, J. (1995). ArtStreet: Joining community through art. *Art Therapy: Journal of the American Art Therapy Association, 12*(2), 184.

Vick, R. M. (2003). In C. A. Malchiodi, *Handbook of art therapy.* New York: Guilford Press.

Vonnegut, K. (1998). *Timequake.* Berkley, CA: Berkley Publications.

Wadeson, H. (1980). *Art psychotherapy.* New York: Wiley & Sons.

Wadeson, H., Landgarten, H., McNiff, S., Free, K., & Levy, B. (1977). The identity of the art therapist: Professional self-concept and public image. *Proceedings of the 1976 Annual National Conference of the American Art Therapy Association.* Baltimore: American Art Therapy Association.

Webber, A. L., & Rice, T. (1970). *Jesus Christ superstar* [Rock opera]. London: Leeds Music.

Wix, L. (2000). Looking for what's lost: The artistic roots of art therapy: Mary Huntoon. *Art Therapy: Journal of the American Art Therapy Association, 17*(3), 168–176.

Wolf, R. (1990). Visceral learning: The integration of aesthetic and creative process in education and psychotherapy. *Art Therapy: Journal of the American Art Therapy Association, 7*(2) 60–69.

Whyte, D. (1990). *Where many rivers meet.* Langley, WA: Many Rivers Press.

Yalom, I. D. (1980). *Existential psythotherapy.* New York: Basic Books.

Yalom, I. D. (2005). *The theory and practice of group psychotherapy* (5th ed.). New York: Basic Books.

INDEX